BEYOND CONTROL

BEYOND CONTROL

Heart-Centered
Classroom Climate and Discipline

Alan Bandstra

DORDT COLLEGE PRESS

Cover design by Rob Haan
Back cover photograph by Amy Vander Berg
Illustrations by Joseph Hoksbergen
Layout by Carla Goslinga

Dordt College Press   www.dordt.edu/DCPcatalog
498 Fourth Avenue NE
Sioux Center, Iowa, 51250
United States of America

ISBN: 978-1-940567-12-9

Printed in the United States of America

The Library of Congress Cataloguing-in-Publication Data is on
file with the Library of Congress, Washington D.C.

Library of Congress Control Number: 2014950725

For Theron, Diane, and Winerva

TABLE OF CONTENTS

Acknowledgements.. i

Preface.. iii

Part I: Classroom Climate and the Christian Teacher

1 – The Climate Connection....................................... 1

2 – Control Issues 11

3 – Outlook Overhauls 19

Part II: Heart-Centered Teaching

4 – Getting Personal.. 33

5 – Cultivating Community....................................... 45

6 – Confronting the Beasts....................................... 59

Part III: Heart-Centered Discipline

7 – Guiding With Grace 75

8 – Stubborn Patience 85

9 – Calm Authority... 95

10 – One to One.. 107

11 – Uprooting Unkindness...................................... 117

12 – Taming the Elephant... 131

13 – Hope and a Future 145

Index.. 155

ACKNOWLEDGEMENTS

God's gifts aren't always what we want, but they often turn out to be just the thing we needed. So I am thankful for three difficult years of teaching after I thought I had discovered everything there was to know about classroom management and discipline. Even though I didn't exactly appreciate having to rewrite the majority of this book when it was almost finished the first time, I believe it will be much more useful in its current form. I am also thankful for the patience of God, as both my ideas about teaching and my teaching practice will always be in need of refining.

My debt to the people who reviewed the manuscripts and revisions is incalculable. John and Susan Van Dyk, Randy Hilbelink, and Barb Hoekstra, you believed in the project, even before it amounted to anything. Thank you to Beth Bleeker, Karen Christians, and Jander Talen who came onboard later. And thanks to my attentive editor, Kim Van Es. Without the suggestions and encouragement that all of you provided, this book could never have been completed.

Thanks to my wife Jolene for the gentle reminders when I wax too philosophical, and thank you for enduring my seeming absent-mindedness. I apologize for the times you sent me to the freezer in the basement and I came back with stack of papers or a book instead. I was probably thinking about something that needed to be written down.

The teachers of Sioux Center Christian School, both those past and present, have inspired me to continue growing in my love for teaching and for children. Thank you for showing me that every child can learn, no matter how needy or naughty.

Lastly, I want to acknowledge three teachers who will always remain dear to me. Theron Ver Steeg, my brother-in-law, taught at Timothy Christian in Wellsburg, Iowa, for just two years before a short battle with cancer ended his life. Though I never had the opportunity to see him teach, I know that his witty style and intuitive knowledge of personalities worked magic in the classroom. My sister Diane Joy was still in college when her life was taken in a car accident. Her goal of becoming a teacher was never realized in the official sense; nonetheless, she touched innumerable people with her exuberance for life and that zesty singing. Finally, my mother-in-law, Winerva Ver Steeg, was always known as a caring teacher by her students. Yet many more were blessed by her hospitality, her laughter, and more than 50 years of music on the church organ. Winerva's dedication to serving others without seeking acclaim will remain her greatest legacy.

PREFACE

I won't judge the man who said it. He was a great teacher, one of the best I'd had. What he said was the truth, too. "Ron, you've got a bad attitude."

Ron and I had been inseparable through most of grade school. We practically lived on our bikes as we imitated stunts of our idol, the daredevil entertainer Evel Knievel. To people who didn't know him well, Ron was a showoff with an eye for trouble. He did have a sensitive side, though, and it often ventured out if there was no audience to impress.

One time Ron took the heat for a mistake that I had made. We were cruising the sidewalks of the college near his house when I attempted a completely brainless maneuver. On a whim I decided to ride Ron's bike down a series of concrete steps. About half-way, the front of his new chrome headlight shook loose from the jolting of the steps and popped off. Remorsefully, we walked our bikes back home, with the interior of his light swinging from a tangle of copper wire.

Ron's grandfather, who lived a couple of houses up the road, had given him the light. Knowing he would find out sooner or later anyway, we decided to stop there first. As we approached the door, Ron turned and looked at me. "Don't say anything; just let me talk," he said. Inside Ron told his grandfather that he had broken his own light. Guilty as could be and scared speechless, I stood by the kitchen table and watched as that old man bawled out my friend.

As we grew up the problems became more serious. Ron's parents went through a divorce. He got into more trouble at school and later with the law. Somewhere along the way our friendship went stale, and after that I saw only the side of him that most people saw, the unruly side.

So privately I concurred with the junior high teacher who publicly announced one day that Ron's biggest problem was his attitude. Who could miss the dark cloud he carried with him everywhere, the shadow that hung over any activity he was involved in? The darkness didn't look like hurt; it looked more like spite, though I imagine now that there was more going on inside than what met the eye. I saw it then the way the teacher saw it. If Ron would only change his attitude, he wouldn't hate school or get into so much trouble. Unfortunately, though the teacher's remark defined the problem, his approach did not solve it. Ron's attitude remained as it was.

Having taught now for several years, I understand the power that attitudes can hold over students and situations. I've enjoyed agreeable kids, who showed respect for me and for their classmates, who took an interest in learning and responded well to discipline. Those students made me feel competent, like I was meant to be a teacher.

Yet I've also worked in classrooms that reeked with negativity and defiance. Like you, perhaps, I have had students who showed little respect for me, who bullied their classmates, bucked the rules, or refused to connect with their learning. In those circumstances it's not just misbehavior that turns a teacher's mouth to cotton or pushes one's blood pressure to the boiling point. Instead, it is the spirit that drives the behavior, something less tangible than actions themselves yet more potent in its effect.

Problems like negativity, defiance, maliciousness, and indifference seem beyond the realm of our control, and that lack of control is frustrating. Whereas we can set limits on complaining, disobeying, and bullying (the *outgrowths* of attitudes) through classroom management plans and discipline systems, it's pointless to devise a rule against an attitude itself.

So what's the use of bothering with what happens inside of students? Why not just focus on the outward behavior and ignore what drives it? For one, treating the cause usually yields better results than treating only the symptoms. If there existed a way to swap an unpleasant attitude with something more positive, the change would produce better behavior and reduce the need for discipline. In addition, teachers influence the attitudes of students, whether they choose to or not. Our approach to classroom management and discipline either reinforces a wayward spirit or nudges it in a more positive direction. Attempting to correct only the misbehavior, without considering what motivated it, can actually spawn more misbehavior.

Another reason to pay attention to attitudes is that they often hold substantial power over the thinking and feelings of others. Just a few students can influence the personality of an entire class, stirring up stink among classmates or sparking animosity between a group and the teacher. Mere mischief isn't always the real culprit, is it? Some kids are naughty, and yet they're still fun to work with. Others follow the rules and still manage to create all sorts of friction.

Finally, the spirit behind our actions and words is closely tied to our beliefs and hopes. For this reason, teachers who care about the direction of their students' hearts can't help but concern themselves with what lies beneath the deeds and misdeeds. The outlook or convictions that a student holds are as important as the way that person behaves.

My original purpose for this book was to create a guide for classroom management and discipline from a Christian perspective. Whereas the book still speaks to classroom management issues, it now recognizes that some of the greatest challenges of teaching require more than an effective classroom management plan. Management focuses on outward behavior; it's about what we can usually control through clear rules and consistent discipline. The idea of classroom climate ventures beyond what can be controlled yet still demands our attention. Classroom climate does not eliminate the need for classroom management, but it does create a context in which we can manage and discipline more effectively, with the hope of encouraging not just outward obedience but a change of heart. If you are reading this book, you likely care about the deepest level of students, their hearts. By the grace of the Spirit, this book may help you in your journey.

PART ONE:
CLASSROOM CLIMATE
AND THE CHRISTIAN TEACHER

CHAPTER ONE:
THE CLIMATE CONNECTION

Personal Problems

Though the people in town were friendly enough, the welcome they gave me was kind of unsettling. Anyone who was connected with the school reacted in about the same way when I introduced myself as the new sixth-grade homeroom teacher. Somehow everyone seemed to know about that class. People I met would laugh and then wish me luck or promise to keep me in their prayers. There were stories about pranks the class had pulled and accounts of teachers who had nearly lost their wits. It was enough to make me wonder about what I had actually signed myself up to do.

One morning before the school year began, a man who had been painting in the building walked into my room, the top of his cap brushing the header of the door as he passed through. With squinting eyes he smiled and slipped off his glove to shake my hand. The gentleman explained that he was a teacher in a nearby high school and that he was also the father of one of my students. He asked if he could have a few minutes to talk about his son.

I was too nervous to think of offering him a chair, so we stood by the bulletin board I had been working on, the stapler hanging open in my hand. Sensing that his height must have seemed intimidating, he shifted his weight to one leg and continued to smile as he shared that his son was into cars, sports, and rock music. The boy was also tall for his age and thought of himself as a lady's man. Still grinning, the dad told me that his son was "cocky," and that he would probably challenge my authority once in awhile. He offered a few suggestions about how to respond when this kind of thing happened and handed me a card with his telephone number, expecting that I would need to call him eventually.

Wow! Through his perspective as a teacher on the one hand and his wisdom as a parent on the other, that painter understood far more about young people than I did at the time. No doubt he knew about the class's reputation, and he understood that his son had played a role in forming that reputation. But this conversation was not about the mob; it was about a person, a young man who was captivated by Mustangs and basketball and his emerging sexuality. The boy's bold personality created a unique set of obstacles for school success, and a certain kind of guidance would be helpful in overcoming those obstacles.

At the time, though, I didn't get it. Inexperienced and probably a little immature, I hadn't the foggiest notion of what the guy was talking about. My problem was a "personal" one. When the school year began, I could not see 29 persons sitting in front of me. Instead, as I looked out from behind my podium, I saw the horde, a collective personality. En masse, they were an entity, a creature with an intimidating life of its own.

Fair to Partly Crabby

The first time it happened was about the third week of September. An off-balance box fan rattled in one corner and another oscillating one rocked as it turned back and forth in the other. Together they kept the body odor in the room from settling but offered little relief from the heat. The vibration of those fans added to the hum of the students who buzzed like flies before a change in the weather. Even when they weren't talking they made noise, a constant drone that you couldn't pinpoint to one person or even to a section in the classroom. Papers rattled, pencils tapped, and bodies shifted in chairs.

Their chatting, though, was almost as incessant as the hum. I had never imagined that a group of students could be so free with their words. The way they talked with each other during my lessons was frustrating enough, but the thing that really got to me was the way they challenged the things I said in class or the consequences I gave when students misbehaved.

Up to this point I had survived by finding ways to keep them busy. They seemed to quiet down when they copied things from the board, so I gave a lot of notes. An assertive discipline system was my strategy for keeping the talking under control. When students spoke out of turn, I wrote their names on the board. If they talked again, I added check marks behind their names. A second check for any student resulted in a detention.

The problem with the assertive system was that consistency seemed impossible. Students who blurted out answers didn't always get their names on the board; it just didn't seem right to punish them for wanting to participate. But then the loud ones, whose names were already on the board, would argue with me about people who talked but didn't get punished. "Ah, come *on!*" "Yeah, *that* ain't fair!"

A few more checkmarks quieted the noise but jacked up the electricity in the atmosphere. The air felt hot and close, despite the fans. A storm was brewing and it was headed our way. Lightning bolts were already firing off in my mind, and I could almost hear the thunder. The anger, truth be known, was one part irritation and three parts anxiety. I was aggravated by the noise and lack of respect, but worse, I was afraid of losing control. My reputation as a teacher was on the line. If I didn't do something soon, the people in town would be telling stories about the new teacher.

Students who maxed out their checks in the name system several times were now treating the whole discipline plan like a joke. Two checks became a license to talk for the rest of the period, and detentions were badges of honor. I don't remember who eventually said the remark or committed the wrongdoing that set me off, but once the squall hit, there was no stopping it. Some of my scolding speech was planned and some of it was just random. The yelling relieved my stress, though, and restored an appearance of order. No one spoke until the class left my room for recess.

Though they were subdued for the rest of that day, their inhibitions didn't last long. The boldest ones were the first to reemerge from their shells, and the others soon followed. I resorted to anger more often, but the effects were shorter lived. My first few outbursts achieved an illusion of control, but in reality they revealed my lack of control.

Eventually my rage became amusing to the students, and they began to look for ways to set me off. Some of the stunts they pulled were actually pretty creative. Take the surprise in the Bible skit, for example, where Ehud stabbed the fat king Eglon and a balloon full of red water in the man's belly emptied onto the floor as he convulsed and died. Today I might have even been able to laugh at something like that, while watching the boys mop up the mess they had made, of course. But I possessed neither the confidence nor the experience to see beyond the disruptions. Instead, a classroom full of rowdies was the only picture my brain could interpret. This gang had done other teachers in, and now they were getting the best of me. I was caught in a cycle—a "cyclone" if you will—a relentless whirl of acting and reacting. My students were beyond control, and it was the longest year of my life.

From Technique to Climate

What a slow learner I was! The next class was not as wild by reputation as their predecessors, but they had heard stories about me. Soon they developed their own style of exasperating, and I endured another long and stressful year. It wasn't until my third year of teaching that I landed upon a seemingly brilliant idea of using rewards and incentive plans instead of punishments and threats. To my satisfaction, the positive reinforcement cut down on the discipline situations and improved the general mood of the classroom. Yet, much of the time I was still disappointed. Some students, working for rewards, would only do the minimum that was required to get the "goodie." Others, who did not find the incentives attractive or who did not think that they could meet the standard, refused to even try. Furthermore, I began to spend so much time keeping track of "payments" and "credits" that the actual work of teaching seemed like a second job.

As time progressed I continued on a quest for the right management system—various combinations of discipline procedures and incentive plans. Some of these systems were successful, but they weren't producing the kinds of attitudes and behaviors I was hoping for. I had learned how to get my students under control, but the way students perceived authority and learning in general were still beyond my control.

Eventually I began to realize that effective classroom management, and the attitudes it fosters, does not rise out of a certain technique or the right bag of tricks. It happens within a climate that teachers intentionally and skillfully create. Climate-sensitive teachers don't eradicate punishments and rewards from their repertoire, but they do realize that getting sincere cooperation from students depends on much more than coercing and coaxing.

What Does Your Climate Grow?

It's easiest to understand the idea of classroom climate when we compare it to the way climates work on earth. We know that "climate" refers to the prevailing conditions of the atmosphere or the "average weather" of a region. Elements such as temperature and precipitation factor into each kind of climate that exists. However, climates are also classified according to the kinds of vegetation that grow in the conditions they create. Each kind of climate encourages certain forms of life to flourish while it makes living difficult for other organisms.

In Iowa, for instance, we have to coddle our lawns to keep them alive. We give them food in the spring and water through the dry months of summer. Every spring we walk around our yard and reseed patches smothered by wet leaves or by ice that stayed around too long in March or even April. Interestingly, the dandelions and thistles love it here; they grow without any extra help. In other places on earth, different climates encourage different kinds of life. Some of the finest wines I have tasted were produced from grapes in Central California and in the Yakima Valley of Eastern Washington where the days are hot and rain is scarce. And recently I was told that the only place in the world to get decent hair for violin bows is Siberia, where the air is so cold that horses don't need to use their tails as fly swatters.

We think about climate on earth, then, in terms of what it is (substance) and what it does (effect). The substance of a climate is the pattern of weather conditions associated with that climate. Classroom climate can also be defined as a set of conditions. While those conditions include the management systems that may be in place, they encompass a great deal more than any one technique or strategy. The way teachers relate to their students and the ways students relate to each other are key factors in the climate of a classroom. The views teachers hold toward learning and the methods they use to evaluate are other factors. Finally, the way that discipline is carried out also greatly affects the climate of a classroom.

Those factors are the *substance* of classroom climate. Yet, when we talk about the climate of a classroom, we are also concerned about what will grow in that climate, the *effect*. As we will see in Chapter Two, when teachers focus only on the behaviors of students, they forget what lies beneath those behaviors. In addition to concerning themselves with how students act, climate-sensitive teachers pay attention to the attitudes of students. They realize how closely the outward behavior is tied to the inward attitudes.

Most dictionaries associate three ideas with the word *attitude*. I've built on each of these ideas for the purpose of fleshing out some meaning to classroom climate. First, an attitude is an opinion, a point of view. It begins with the way that people see or perceive what happens to them or what goes on around them. Second, an attitude is a general feeling about what people perceive. In other words, an attitude is more than just a perspective; it is interwoven with the emotions. Finally, attitudes have an influence on the way people conduct themselves, on the way they behave.

Let's say I am a student who harbors the perception that my teacher doesn't like me. That impression is based largely on what I *see*. The teacher points out my mistakes but never seems to notice when I try my best. My perception is likely to bring about certain *feelings* toward that teacher: resentment and defensiveness, for example. Furthermore, my perception and feelings are going to influence the way I *act* around this teacher or the way that I respond when she confronts me about something I have done wrong.

In addition to the seeing-feeling-behaving interpretations, I would like to add a fourth dimension. Attitudes are also shaped by what we *believe* to be true. A student who believes that the teacher is spiteful will tend to notice only those actions which support that presumption, while one who regards a teacher as kind will notice the actions that affirm that opinion. I'd like to call this fourth component of attitude the *trust* dimension. A positive attitude signifies that a person trusts in someone or something. Conversely, a person who displays a negative attitude most likely does not trust the person or the thing to which that attitude is directed. In an immediate sense, students who trust their teacher are more likely to demonstrate a positive attitude toward that teacher than students who don't. Ultimately, though, the trust component is about more than having faith in one's teacher. We will return to this concept in Chapter Three.

A "heart-centered" classroom climate focuses on all four aspects of attitude. Whereas the physical heart pumps blood through the body, the heart can also be thought of as the center of a person's perceptions, feelings, and trust. It's the origin of what a person says and does. *A heart-centered climate attempts to influence the attitudes students have toward authority and toward each other, toward learning and correction.*

In the cultivating or reshaping of attitudes, climate-sensitive teaching often yields—or grows—more desirable behaviors. I like the metaphor of "growing" different attitudes because it honors the truth that something wholly (or Holy) other than ourselves is at work. As any farmer or gardener knows, humans can only create the optimum conditions for growth; we cannot "make" a thing germinate or flourish. Similarly, as we focus our efforts on the hearts of individuals, we recognize that God's Spirit is the One who ultimately brings about a change.

Comparing classroom climate to the idea of climate on earth is one way to make sense of the way classroom climate works. There is another angle that is important to consider, though. The term *classroom atmosphere* is commonly used interchangeably with classroom climate. This expression itself is rich with meaning.

Atmosphere and Appetite

A bowl of rice at R and G's Lounge in Chinatown tastes about the same as the bowl of rice I can order at the fast-food Asian restaurant six blocks from my house. Yet on a recent trip to San Francisco, I was willing to pay a significantly higher price for the food because of the atmosphere. The traditional Oriental menu items like shark fin soup and jade rabbit sea cucumber, the simple elegant place settings, the guests and waiters speaking to each other in Chinese—all of these elements affirmed that this was authentic—real.

While the right atmosphere enhances the eating, you know that a bad atmosphere can spoil it if you've ever eaten with the stench of something rotten in the air or paid for service that was lousy. Taste appeal means little if you have to swat flies while you eat or sit near people who chew with their mouths open. Offensive odors, rudeness, and grubbiness spoil food more quickly than noxious bacteria.

To get at this other aspect of classroom climate sometimes referred to as classroom atmosphere, it helps to compare food and setting with school work and classroom context. Just as the air we breathe affects our craving for food, the atmosphere of a classroom can whet the appetite for learning or churn the stomach. I used to tutor a seventh grader from another school whose mission focused more on filtering out the bad than proclaiming or celebrating the good. Though a school-wide discipline plan kept outward disrespect and fighting to a minimum, many of the students didn't genuinely respect authority or get along well together. The teachers either ignored or failed to notice that Julie had no friends, nor did they see how this problem affected her ability to learn. It made no difference in her life that biblical principles were faithfully taught at weekly chapels and in daily devotions. Julie detested school and everything it stood for.

The foul atmosphere in that place snuffed out Julie's desire for two aspects of learning. One was content learning. She despised history, science, math, and language. If Julie acquired any concepts at all, it was only through force feeding. She learned for a grade—or to keep the teachers off her back. In addition to her distaste for schoolwork, Julie also began to develop an aversion to the spiritual aspect of learning. As words about God or living the godly life intermingled with the stench of an uncaring atmosphere, the result was an apathetic attitude. It wasn't that she was slipping down a slippery slope toward atheism; she just lost interest. During a time of life when her soul was especially needful for the presence of God and the truths of his Word, Julie remained underfed in a learning institution where she could have been nourished.

My belief that Christ is king over all of creation has led me to teach in a Christian school. Christ has something to say about how we interpret the information we learn and how we apply the skills we develop. A Christian perspective or point of view in every teaching unit is foundational to the mission of our school. However, the sovereignty of Christ does not begin and end with the head knowledge students acquire. He also lays claim to the context in which that knowledge is presented. Without an atmosphere that communicates the love of Christ, quality Christian teaching is an eight-course banquet served downwind from a cesspool.

On the positive side, classroom atmosphere is a way that the Spirit of Christ can pervade all of our teaching and interacting, even when the name of Christ is not to be heard or seen. Christian educators in public institutions, generally speaking, may not share their faith in class or overtly teach from a Christian point of view. And, though I could, I also do not talk about God in every lesson. I take advantage of moments and situations that lend themselves to sharing eternal truths, but forcing "Christian talk" into every discussion cheapens the message and turns listeners off to its life-changing power. Hubertus Halbfas says it well:

> To talk about God you do not have to use theological terms.... It is not the "what" that gives human language (religious) "content," but its "how." Some people just speak about children, their house and garden, supper and bed, and yet their discourse is full of faith and hope, thanks and prayer. Others, of course, talk in a highly learned, theological manner, using the kind of concepts that would make you think they were on

intimate terms with the Holy Trinity. But what does that kind of talk produce? Emptiness, helplessness, and often anger.... The "content" of religious discourse is "God," but it is not this word, together with [Christian vocabulary], that communicates God, but only the life-revealing language of other human beings.[1] (119-120)

These ideas are not intended to suggest that references to God's name or the Christian faith are to be squelched in a Christian school. On the contrary, their timely use is crucial. The point is that a truly Christ-centered education includes more than simply the kind of language teachers employ. It permeates the "air" students breathe, as well as the knowledge they are fed. A Spirit-breathed approach affects the classroom atmosphere and subsequently the classroom climate.

Conclusion

So far we have seen that attitudes are "grown," or at least encouraged, within the climate of a classroom. Climate is the overall spirit that drives the teaching, interacting, and the correction of misbehavior. A healthy classroom atmosphere provides a context for teaching about God and living in his world. The context of the words spoken about faith has an influence on whether students will learn to love that faith and live it in their lives.

If we are concerned about attitudes, we should think about the ways we motivate students to behave or to learn and about how we should deter them from wrong. Some strategies for teaching and discipline create conditions that seem to grow negative attitudes. Let's move forward to take a look at the issue of control.

---

1 Dykstra, C. (2005). *Growing in the life of faith, education and Christian practices.* Louisville: Westminster: John Knox Press, second edition.

CHAPTER 2:
CONTROL ISSUES

Kitty Control

When I was ten or so, my sisters and I thought it would be fun to put on an animal circus. The show would feature our farm cats, who were always willing to go along with things if they caught wind that food was involved. After scrounging through a few junk piles for useful items, we built an obstacle course, a series of six or seven stunts that the cats would need to learn for the show.

Table scraps would serve as the lure. Human leftovers were always enticing to the cats on our farm whose regular diet consisted of Puppy Chow, which they shared with the dog, or occasional mice if they found the motivation to go hunting. Using small pieces of the food, we began coaxing them up a miniature ladder, across a balance beam, then onto the trapeze. At first we meted out a reward each time one completed a single step in the routine. Then the food came only after a cat performed a series of stunts consecutively. We were amazed at how quickly our pets learned all of the tricks and how eager they were to repeat them for such small pay. As a matter of fact, a couple of days after we'd lost interest in the circus and moved on to other pursuits, the cats would still run over to the course and start their routines whenever they saw us walk out of the house.

Of course the term *behavior modification* was completely unknown to us, but the idea behind our achievement with the cats was as fascinating as it was simple: almost complete kitty control lay in those little scraps of bread!

If an animal needed to be redirected, however, then a different kind of conditioning, other than rewards, sometimes became necessary. Our neighbor's dog Siesel, for example, was into extreme pickup chasing. The other cars that came through the neighborhood were all fun targets for him, but Dad's old Ford put out the ultimate thrill. Its crumbling muffler was loud, and one of the rusty quarter panels rattled whenever Dad hit the gas. Siesel's ears could pick up the sound of our truck when it left home across the section, and by the time we rounded the corner, he was already hurtling up the road to meet us, baring his teeth and barking himself into a frenzy. The dog would bite at the moving wheels and sometimes even run underneath the pickup as it clattered by. His game was more than just dangerous; it was suicidal. And someday Siesel would probably have gotten himself killed if Dad hadn't scared him into quitting.

One morning, on his way past Siesel's place, Dad decided to give the hound a little surprise. He waited until Siesel was next to the rear of the pickup, then shut off the engine and quickly restarted it. Doing so causes a small explosion in the exhaust system known as *backfire*, which usually registers about five decibels louder than a shotgun blast.

Just about everything worked perfectly. There was a huge "Ka-bang," even louder than normal! The noise sent a shocked and bewildered Siesel somersaulting right off the road and into the ditch. As soon as his feet made contact with the ground again, they were kicking up clouds of dust as he sped across the field like a screaming bullet.

However, one part of the plan "backfired," you might say. The discharge, which was a little more than Dad was aiming for, blew a hole about the size of a grapefruit in the bottom of the muffler, and his once moderately loud pickup now sounded like a stock car. The ultimate goal was achieved, though. Siesel developed a new respect for our pickup. From then on, he continued to bark at us as we passed by, but he always did so within safe reach of his mulberry grove.

Kiddy Control

The cat circus was fun, in part, because it sent us on a kind of power trip to be in control, to make other living things carry out a purpose that we had devised. To be sure, rewarding benefited the cats as well, but ultimately, the rewards served our own agenda. Through minimal effort we placed ourselves in a position of control.

Backfiring Siesel was more than just for fun, though we did get kind of a bang out of his reaction. The nobler cause of sparing life was Dad's primary reason for scaring him. I'm sure that if one of us had sat down, looked Siesel in the eye, and lectured him on the hazards of his behavior, he would have listened politely to the speech—most dogs do when you speak to them directly. But it is also likely that he would have promptly ignored us once we started up the pickup to drive away. Therefore an association had to be created in Siesel's mind, a connection between his misbehavior and, in this case, a loud scary noise.

I begin with these two stories because they highlight a way of controlling students that I now try to avoid: manipulation. Manipulation can happen in just about any kind of interaction between teachers and students. We'll start with a definition of this word as it relates to teaching and discipline, then show how manipulative management counters a climate which honors Christ and squelches the attitudes desired in a Christian climate.

Manipulative Management and its Consequences

Classroom management becomes manipulative when students' behavior is influenced through enticement or intimidation, serving the teacher's advantage. Manipulation occurs when students are focused on the good things that will happen if they comply with the teacher or the consequences that may happen if they don't. The success of our kitty circus clearly relied on manipulation. The primary motivation for participating was not the activity itself but the food held in front of them. The lure got them to perform an exercise that they would not have chosen to do on their own. Moreover, the activity we were getting them to perform served our own agendas but did not help them in any way, except perhaps a boosted self-esteem through their sense of accomplishment.

Similarly, Siesel the dog was motivated to stop chasing our pickup through a form of manipulation. The stimulus in this case was fear—not fear of what might actually happen to him if he were to continue biting the wheels of a moving vehicle, but fear of the loud noise he began to connect with our truck the day its muffler blew apart next to his face. It could be argued, of course, that in both of these cases, the manipulation was innocent. The cats were not subjected to any pain, and all of them acquired some bonus food in their diet as a result of their cooperation. Siesel's lesson caused him a few moments of displeasure, but in the end it probably saved his life.

Manipulation at school becomes most visible when incentives or threats are used to extract compliance, especially if those tactics serve the teacher's agenda without the students having a clear sense of the meaning of their tasks. When teachers say, "Look at what I got these kids to do for a piece of candy," it sounds like manipulation. Whereas caring teachers may find various ways to celebrate accomplishments with their students, coercion is dehumanizing, especially when that approach dominates a person's teaching style.

Beyond candy (which is the last thing most students need), other common positive control techniques include rewards like stickers, praise, extra free time, and good grades. Popular negative techniques, by contrast, are consequences like scolding, detentions, and low grades.

In ways that are more hidden, manipulation also happens when teachers subtly favor the students who participate often or get involved, who follow the rules and earn good marks. It occurs when teachers respond to misbehavior with sarcasm or cutting remarks, when they seem to withhold love from individuals who make mistakes or who are disobedient.

Of course there are times when coaxing or coercing is needed. I am not entirely against stickers and praise, scoldings and detentions. [1] Though some of the strategies I mentioned may not be "bad" in themselves, it is the attitudes and ideas that drive our techniques, as well as the attitudes and ideas they may foster in our students that we should keep under surveillance. What causes us to sometimes resort to manipulation, and what are the ideas that consequently may begin to grow in our students?

First of all, manipulation can become a shortcut that bypasses the hard work of quality teaching. I tend to rely more heavily on external forms of motivation when I have not invested the time and work that it takes to teach well. Rather than reflecting on learning goals and finding creative ways for the students to reach those goals, I "cover" the material. Sensing my lack of passion for the subject, the students become disinterested, and I resort to punishments and rewards in order to keep the class on track. If manipulation works once, it is easy to continue on this path. Why expend the effort it takes to develop meaningful units and engaging lessons if the students will learn for a reward? Also, if I can get my class to behave appropriately with a reward or a punishment, there is no longer any reason to attempt the more difficult task of teaching how right and wrong affect others and ourselves. Beginning teachers and those new to a school system or grade level often use external motivation since it is difficult to be creative when one is also learning the material for the first time. Having taught in the same place for more than twenty years, however, I have no excuse.

Manipulation also produces in students a wrong idea about learning and a wrong idea about grace. Whether or not the teacher is driven by these ideas, they can still inadvertently become ingrained in the students. Motivational theorist Alfie Kohn, in his book *Punished by Rewards*, speaks about the negative ways that manipulation, especially through rewarding, affects learning.[2] One important point he mentions is that re-

---

1   Though many of the strategies are not bad in themselves, teacher behaviors like favoritism, belittling, and biting sarcasm are to be avoided at all times.

2   Kohn, A. (1993). *Punished by rewards*. Boston: Houghton Mifflin.

warding students for learning turns education into an economy: learning is seen as work that one does in exchange for a payment. At one level, this idea has a profound effect on motivation as students progress through the grades. For example, if the reward is not large enough, the learner will see no reason for doing the work. "Why don't *we* get paid for learning?" my students sometimes ask. "*We're* the ones who do all the *work*." At a deeper and more serious level, the naturally curious side of children, their desire to make sense out of things, or to use their knowledge in a meaningful way is often lost when manipulation turns schooling into an economy. Essentially, learning is demoted via the promotion of the reward. When teachers overemphasize rewards, the underlying message communicated to children goes something like this: "If you endure this negative experience called learning, you can earn preferable things like material possessions and entertainment."

"Reimbursing" students for work (either for working hard in class or for performing classroom chores) also breaks down community. Instead of focusing on the needs of others, for example, students think about what they stand to gain. Beyond self-centeredness, I have also seen reward systems give rise to envy and resentment. One who selflessly performs a task without expecting a payment feels slighted when somebody else is handed a prize for completing a similar task. Another who volunteers to spend his recess organizing the bookshelves wonders why his payment is the same as that of a classmate who gave up only a minute of study time to sort papers for the teacher. The idea of *positive* reinforcement is only partially correct, then. Even though reward systems appear to encourage helpful behavior, they often lead to disgruntlement. Because it is difficult to maintain consistency, positive reinforcement for good behavior can turn students against their teacher and against each other.

Believe it or not, reducing classroom management to punishments and rewards may also affect students' theology. Reformed theologian Scott Hoezee, in his discussion on "Grace and Capitalism," raises another important point about the economizing of education and how it affects students' ideas about grace. When we speak of unconditional grace, on the one hand, while using threats or incentives to get children to comply on the other, we contradict ourselves. We want students to know that, in Christ, God loves them no matter what they do. We want them to be so thankful for God's unmerited kindness that their whole lives reflect gratitude to the Lord. Yet we sometimes favor the ones whose behavior meets our approval. Children learn their lessons for a star, for candy, or for a grade. They might even feel that their hard work will earn them the teacher's love. Misbehaving students, on the other hand, can easily receive the impression that they are loved less than their more obedient counterparts. Hoezee speaks of God's "grace economy" in which the commodity of grace is freely given to all:

> The mystery of this economy is that it manages its goods so poorly! It does not reckon merit; it simply grants grace freely, gloriously, and profusely to anyone whom God chooses. Unlike almost every other economic system we have ever heard of, God's gracious economy—the administration, distribution, and stewardship of God's salvation—is a giveaway[3] (p. 123).

Another issue that Kohn raises about manipulation is that it dehumanizes, as I alluded to earlier. My personal experience concurs with his argument. Exactly how do I take the compliment spoken by a person who wants something from me? If I sense that the praise is insincere, or worse yet, that the giver of praise has an underlying agenda, I am much less eager to find ways to please that person. Equally degrading are criticisms from people who have their own interests in mind or who attempt to cover up their own shortcomings. Controlling types of compliments and critiques are demeaning, says Kohn, because of the way they separate the giver and the receiver: the one who bestows raises himself to a position above the one who receives.

Wait a minute, though. Shouldn't our students be kept in their place? They cannot have the same status as the teacher. As it relates to the idea of authority, this point is legitimate. The teacher needs to be the one in charge. However, in terms of our merits and our weaknesses, all of us are equal before God. None of us is "greater" than any other. Young ones are not elevated to the status of the grown-up; rather we, as adults, are called to lower ourselves, to take on the humble nature of a child. I can't help but think here of the way Jesus once answered his disciples' question about who was the greatest. Calling a little child to his side, he said, "Unless you change and become like little children, you will never enter the kingdom of heaven" (Matthew 18:3, New International Version). Whereas manipulation can raise feelings of resentment, teachers who humble themselves in relation to their students bring honor to Christ. "And whoever welcomes one such child in my name welcomes me" (vs. 5).

Finally, manipulation ignores an element that lies at the core of ev-

---

3 Hoezee, S. (1996). *The riddle of grace: Applying grace to the Christian Life*. Grand Rapids, Michigan: Wm. B. Eerdmans Publishing Company.

ery human being—the heart. As I said in Chapter One, everything we do reflects what occupies our hearts. Ignoring the heart is why a manipulative atmosphere falls short both practically and philosophically. Theoretically speaking, acknowledging that students are humans presumes treating them and responding to them as humans. And practically speaking, if we desire more than surface cooperation, then we have to look below the surface when we attempt to influence their thoughts and behaviors.

A Time for Coercing?

At times, coaxing or coercing may be the best strategy to use in the classroom. I have not yet learned to survive without certain threats or incentives in place, even in classes where a positive attitude is the driving force. Pushing the boundaries, or following my own agenda instead of someone else's, is part of human nature. Here is a case in point. I am not a thief at heart. However, if there were no fines at our local public library, I'd be guilty of keeping the books and movies I borrow long past their due dates. I am aware that there are other people who would like to use those books or movies. However, I am also selfish. Returning items to the library isn't a priority when I have other things to do. So, even for people who mean well, who have a "good" attitude, certain forms of external motivation are needed because we are human.

If students with positive attitudes about learning occasionally need incentives or threats to keep them on track, it's obvious that students with negative attitudes need them as well. There are students in all age groups who lack the maturity to grasp or value the greater good in something, who need some form of external motivation in order to do just about anything. Furthermore, sometimes attitudes are grown "from the outside in." I've seen many students over the years grow to enjoy reading, not just because the librarian made good books available, but because she said, "You must be quiet now and you must read!"

Even though attitudes exist in the realm of influence rather than control, heart-centered teachers still bear a responsibility to use coercion to keep students from wrongful paths. A heart-centered classroom climate cannot exist in a place of chaos anymore than it can exist in a place of manipulation.

Conclusion

Because of human nature, most classrooms do not function effectively without the presence of external motivation or deterrents. However, the type of control we use becomes an issue when threats and incentives dominate the classroom climate. Teachers looking for an easy way out may use external motivation to get students to learn or to cooperate instead of doing the work that it takes to teach well. An overuse or misuse of external motivation leads to misdirected attitudes about learning and about grace: learning is devalued in favor of possessions or pleasure, and love is something to be earned rather than received as a gift in spite of our shortcomings. Finally, manipulation dehumanizes; it treats people like pets. A classroom climate characterized by rewards and punishments may yield some of the desired behaviors, but it circumvents the heart.

Having seen the connections among manipulation, human nature, and attitude, we are now ready to look at the nature of a heart-centered classroom climate.

Chapter 3:
Outlook Overhauls

Bucket of Bolts

When I was in college, one of my summer jobs was to work the night shift at a local window factory. The repetition of assembly line work often produces muscle memory, and turning in screws with a pneumatic drill soon became my personal specialty. One evening the manager came over to tell me that he was transferring me to another work area. A six-hundred-thousand-dollar robot on that line had malfunctioned, and they needed a human fill-in.

This robot was supposed to perform essentially the same job as I had been trained to do: take a window from a stack, turn fourteen screws into the frame and send it down the line for the next application. The technical problem was that the machine had acquired a bit of an attitude. Instead of gently placing each completed window on the conveyor, it would hoist the product as high as it could and then smash it on the floor.

Because this piece of equipment was worth more than half-a-million dollars, I couldn't resist the obvious question of how the new position would affect my wage. The manager, who wasn't known for his sense

of humor, ignored me and explained where he could be found if I had any questions.

It's kind of amusing when mechanical objects act like people, especially since machines cannot actively resist their human operators. Normally, when a machine malfunctions, a certain component in the system is at fault. If the cause can be determined and repaired, the machine will again work in the way it was intended. The defective robot at the window factory wasn't defiant; it was just broken. Eventually the technicians were able to rectify the problem, and I was sent back to my original work area.

Profoundly Human

By contrast, students are able to resist their teachers. One common reason for resistance is a lack of student motivation; the kids just don't want to learn. Some of that segment merely check out or find ways to avoid work, while others seem more "actively unmotivated." They ask why they need to learn the material the teacher is presenting or what real-world use they will have for their school work. On the other hand, some resistance is more relational than motivational. Children may show more fondness for the teacher down the hall than they do for the one standing in front of them. It's easy to feel snubbed by students who outwardly admire other adults in the building. Teachers in this position naturally perceive their students' indifference as resistance. Finally, there is the belligerent sort of resistance. This kind shows itself when students draw teachers into confrontation by finding ways to irritate them or by disregarding their authority. Of course, sometimes various forms of resistance materialize at the same time and feed off one another.

The faulty component in human beings, if you will, is the heart. Human behavior and the mindset that drives it flow out of the heart, yet this heart cannot be extracted and worked on like a piece of equipment in a machine. We have no easy way of getting to the part that needs to be repaired! Another problem, which often amplifies the struggle, is that student resistance tends to affect our own outlook and decision making.

Research on motivation confirms the symbiotic relationship teachers and students have on each other's outlook and behavior. In 1993, Skinner and Belmont conducted a study on teacher behavior that fosters the fulfillment of basic psychological needs in students, specifically the need to be competent, autonomous, and related to other people. According to their model, the teacher practice of providing structure (information about desired outcomes, help and support where needed, and clear, consistent feedback) helps students to feel competent. The teacher behavior of providing autonomy support (allowing children the freedom to determine their own behavior by providing choices and by minimizing external forms of control) fulfills the basic human need to be autonomous. The teacher behavior that provides for relatedness is involvement (taking time to develop positive relationships with students and allowing learners to connect with their peers). When these basic psychological needs are met, students are more motivated to learn.[1]

Whereas Skinner and Belmont confirmed that teacher behavior does influence students' perceptions and students' engagement, their study focused on more than just the effects of teacher behavior on students. They also investigated the ways that student behavior affects teachers. One of the tendencies they found was a reciprocal effect in student motivation on teacher behavior:

> Teachers respond to children who have initially high behavioral engagement with more involvement, more autonomy support, and even to a degree, more contingency and consistency, and they respond to children who are more passive with correspondingly more neglect, coercion, and inconsistency. Because these supports have an impact on children's subsequent engagement, this means that children who have high behavioral engagement are treated in a way that is likely to increase their active participation in class, whereas teachers deal with children who have lower behavioral engagement in a way that will exacerbate their initial passivity and withdrawal from learning activities. (578)

The causes for these trends are not difficult to explain. Skinner and Belmont point out that student passivity makes teachers feel incompetent or disliked. As a result, teachers will like apathetic students less and spend less time with them. In addition, because passive students appear to be unmotivated, teachers often respond to passivity with more external pressure, which tends to result in more disengagement. It seems that as a general rule, when negativity or disengagement rears its head, teachers feed the beast. They allow the attitudes of students (their perceptions, emotions, and behavior) to affect their own teacher outlook and behavior, which, in turn results in more student disengagement.

I would like to think that heart-centered teachers are immune to this propensity, but my own track record proves otherwise. Further, from what I have gathered in conversations with other teachers, not many of us are resistant to the bug. As heart-centered teachers, we may be even more

1 Skinner, E. A. & Belmont, M. J. (1993). Motivation in the classroom: reciprocal effects of teacher behavior and student engagement across the school year. *Journal of Educational Psychology, 85,* 571-581.

susceptible to the influence of student attitude because we want students not only to learn but to find meaning in learning. We want them not only to stay out of trouble but to love the good. When student resistance clouds our vision, two different responses are common. Sometimes we get into a funk, questioning our ability to teach or even doubting our worth as persons. Or we become vindictive, lashing out at kids without really thinking about the resentment our anger may cause. Of course these two seemingly opposite reactions often go hand in hand. When I feel crummy about myself, for example, I get defensive and snap back at students more quickly than I do when I feel confident. Whether the reaction is gloominess or vindictiveness, however, the problem is the same. Instead of providing guidance to students headed in the wrong direction, we allow them to bear a negative influence over us; we lose track of our role as teachers.

Part of the problem is that we are too short-sighted. It's difficult to lead students with critical or defiant attitudes because we have trouble seeing beyond what is directly in front of us: their behavior. What we need is something to focus on that is bigger and more solid than the apparent hopelessness of the here-and-now.

In Chapter One we saw that a person's outlook is commonly thought of as an outgrowth of one's perceptions and feelings: the way we see and feel about things affects the way we behave. In addition, we saw that what people believe to be true also affects their view of reality. As I pointed out in that earlier discussion, a prerequisite in growing new attitudes is gaining the trust of one's students.

Since we are focusing on a teacher's outlook, though, let's consider the way this concept applies to us. If our own attitudes about teaching and about students are shaped as much by what we *don't see* as they are shaped by what we *do see*, then we really ought to spend a few moments focusing on our beliefs and their implications. For example, what do we presume about human nature? How were we designed to function? If we aren't hitting the mark, what has gone wrong? And is there anything that can be done to repair us or to get us back on course?

A Story to Live By
Perhaps you've noticed by now that I love stories. Stories give meaning to our experiences; they help us to interpret the material of our lives. My view of heart-centered teaching and discipline has been shaped by the narrative of scripture and its themes of creation, fall, and redemption.[2]

---

2 Wolters, A. M. (1985). *Creation regained: biblical basis for a Christian worldview.*

Returning to this narrative—where it's been and where it is ultimately headed—keeps me grounded amid some of the greatest challenges of teaching. A look at some of these themes will provide a backdrop for the rest of this book.

At the culmination of his creating work, God could have made beings who would merely serve and obey him, like robots or automatons behaving according to a set of preprogrammed instructions. Instead he created people with a capacity to experience, to respond to his world. He gave them intelligence and emotions to connect with their experiences, and he granted them the ability to act according to their thoughts and feelings. In addition, he designed humans to live in relationship. They were to exist in relationship with God, with each other, and with the creation.[3]

These relationships were not to be driven by control, as in the connection between engineer and machine. The dynamic force was love. People would worship God and enjoy his presence in their daily lives, adhering to the limits he set for them. They would delight in each other and share themselves with each other. Finally, they would take pleasure in the creation and care for it. Whereas God eventually did command people to serve and to obey, these actions were to be rooted in love—expressions of gratitude.

God provided everything people might have wanted. They could have enjoyed him and his gifts forever if they would have trusted him. Instead, through temptation, they were swayed to believe that God was holding out on them, that there was something else to be gained apart from what he had provided. Their choice to make decisions apart from God's will ushered sin into the world. It is important to note here that sin is not a separate entity in creation. Sin cannot exist on its own; rather, it acts as a parasite, breaking or distorting every part of God's good world.[4] Hence, people cannot be sorted into categories of good or bad. Each person and each aspect of creation retains part of the "good" that the Creator designed into it, but it no longer functions solely according to God's original intent.

Sin brought brokenness to the relationships that people were in, turning love inward. Instead of worshiping God and enjoying his presence, people now tend to worship the things he gave to them. Instead of

Grand Rapids, Michigan: Wm. B. Eerdmans Publishing Co.

3   Fennema, J. (2005). *The religious nature and biblical nurture of God's children.* Sioux Center, Iowa: Dordt College Press.

4   Wolters, A. M. Ibid.

delighting in and caring for others, people began to think first of themselves. This theme is exemplified as different people throughout history take turns playing roles in the story. Those who make choices according to their own limited perspectives or their own desires create problems for themselves and for others.

As the story of the fall plays out, however, the story of redemption also begins to unfold. Sometimes God allows people to suffer the consequences of their actions in the hope that they will return to him; other times he rescues them from their predicaments and gives them a fresh start. Eventually, God's redemptive work reaches its climax in the work of his Son, Jesus Christ.

I find it somewhat ironic that Christ came to earth to establish a new kingdom but spent most of his time talking about it instead of fighting for it. If history serves as a pattern, the typical way of building a kingdom had almost always involved moving into a region with one's military forces, overpowering the defenses, and taking control of the area. This is certainly the kind of physical kingdom many of Jesus' followers were looking for as they suffered under the tyranny of imperial Rome. Even though many eventually recognized him as the promised descendant of King David whose throne would last forever, in his earthly ministry Christ never assumed the posture of a traditional monarch or even a warrior; he was primarily a rabbi—a teacher.

In his teaching, which Jesus delivered both through speaking and through his way of life, we learn that the kingdom itself is somewhat of an irony. It's not about getting ahead but about helping others. Those considered blessed are not the assertive and the strong-armed but the meek and the peacemakers, the ones who show mercy instead of revenge. All of his commands boil down to one main rule: love one another.

The greatest and most wonderful irony in Christ's redemptive work is seen in his death on the cross. Because people chose to trust in their own way and to place themselves at the center, a penalty needed to be paid. Instead of forcing people to suffer the consequences of their choices, though, God himself became the atoning sacrifice for sin, through the God-human Jesus Christ. The Head of God's kingdom served the penalty for his subjects' rebellion, with his own blood!

As amazing as this truth is, however, the cross is about more than a one-time payment for sin. Jesus said that if people would be his disciples, they must deny themselves and take up their own cross. This statement does not mean that the penalty for sin must be paid again in some other way. Taken in the context of his overall message, the call signifies that "cross-bearing" is the way through which Christ's kingdom comes about. His kingdom grows when followers of Christ deny their own desires for the sake of others, when they forgive people who hurt or annoy them instead of getting even. Theologian N. T. Wright describes the centrality of the cross:

> When we speak of "following Christ," it is the crucified Messiah we are talking about. His death was not simply the messy bit that enables our sins to be forgiven but that can then be forgotten. The cross is the surest, truest, and deepest window on the very heart and character of the living and loving God; the more we learn about the cross, the more we discover about the One in whose image we are made and hence about our own vocation to be...cross-bearing people, the people in whose lives and service the living God is made known. (94-95)[5]

Finally, Christ claimed the victory over death in rising from the grave. Yet in this great triumphal act, Christ also prevailed over that which brings death. In other words, Christ's resurrection offers further benefits than a guarantee for eternal life after we leave this world. As Pastor Ken Baker puts it, "The fact that Christ was raised from the dead was the ultimate game-changer for a world gripped by the power of death— not just death as life's last move, but in the biblical sense of a pervasive power that drags life down."[6] In rising from the dead, Christ set people free to live by way of the kingdom, turning love outward, acting in mercy instead of revenge. Though this kingdom has not yet come in its fullness, we see evidence of it today where people worship God and obey his will, where they serve others and care for the creation.

Attitude Adjustment

What does the story mean for us as heart-centered teachers? As I suggested in the beginning of this chapter, it doesn't take much experience in working with young people to realize that humans are broken. Yet it's also clear that working toward restoration in people is dicey business. In the first place, we can't just tinker others back into a correct working order because we have no direct access to the thing that needs repairing, namely the heart. Secondly, certain kinds of brokenness in people seem to amplify our own flaws as human beings. When teachers meet with resistance in students, for example, we tend to behave in ways that intensify

5   Wright, N. T. (1999). *The challenge of Jesus: Rediscovering who Jesus was and is.* Downers Grove, Illinois: InterVarsity Press.

6   Baker, K. (2012, April). Practicing resurrection where it matters most. *The Banner, 147,* 20-21.

the opposition instead of turning it around.

For teachers who follow Christ, the surest way out of this pattern is to put more stock in the faith aspect of our outlook, to recall that we're part of a bigger narrative. When our view of reality is shaped by scripture, we begin to see our students and their behavior differently. A shift also occurs in the way we perceive ourselves and our roles in working with young people. We will spend a few moments now looking at classroom climate and discipline in the light of the themes we have just surveyed. Each of these implications will be developed further in the chapters that follow.

Created and Fallen

One point that we need to recall at the outset is that sin cuts through everything and everyone. Whereas some students present more of a challenge to work with than others, we can't sort them into categories of good kids and bad kids. All of us were designed to function according to God's will, and each of us is affected by the fall. Most of the snags teachers run into with student resistance come from a failure to account either for the manner in which God has created them or for the way that sin affects them.

If we believe, for example, that humans are fashioned with the capacity to reason and to experience emotions, then the traditional way of viewing learners as empty heads to be filled is insufficient. Instead of seeing education as something that is done *to* students, we realize that they were designed to be active participants in their learning. Further, though not everyone will always find meaning or enjoyment in their learning, teachers can still work toward meeting these human needs in their instructional strategies. Both the ways we engage students in their study and the degree to which they should assume ownership depend on their maturity, of course; but at every level students can be seen as contributors to a learning community. Treating them as mere containers to be stocked with knowledge and skills is dehumanizing and often leads to resistance.

Accounting for the created nature of students also includes seeing and honoring their uniqueness, though the term "unique" is somewhat inadequate. I prefer "original," which reminds me that each person is a completely new creation, purposefully designed by God—not merely a random product of genetic alignment. God does not mass produce; he creates! In each student we see an origin—a beginning of something that has never occurred before. We notice gifts and ideas that come to expression in ways unparalleled by anyone else. Looking for the good in kids who cause trouble is not a habit most of us fall into naturally; yet it's a requirement for anyone who prefers guiding wayward students over fighting them.

As we saw earlier, sin turns the focus inward instead of outward. It is often this self-referenced state-of-heart that confronts us when we encounter resistance or negative attitudes. Yet teachers compound the problem when they forget that students were created to exist in relationships that are driven by love and not control. I can't help but think here of the attempt to "program" young people into a proper way of behaving through a heavy reliance on punishments and rewards. We examined this concept at length in the last chapter, but an additional point becomes clear in light of the current discussion. Threats and incentive plans encourage the student to ask, "How does my behavior affect my own well-being?" instead of, "How does my behavior affect the people around me?"

Lastly, ignoring the connection between human nature and attitudes also magnifies the inward focus of students. Let me explain. Each of us perceives reality differently because of the "originality" that I spoke of a moment ago. Further, any two of us who see or experience the same event can feel entirely differently about it. Finally, even when we possess the same emotions, we often respond or react to those feelings in different ways. Our attitudes, you see, are remarkably unique to who we are. Because they are so deeply personal, we instinctively protect them. There is little that provokes more resistance to someone else's guidance than to be treated as though one's own reasoning or feelings count for nothing.

Redeemed and Restored

When self-willed students begin to play on our nerves, our natural tendency as sinful human beings is to respond in the same way that those students behave toward us. Breaking free of this habit requires another look at the kingdom of Christ, a kingdom that values others above self and grows through love and sacrifice instead of control or revenge. Our role within this kingdom is to practice restoration, to help young people function again in the way God intended. These ideas sound nice, of course, but I know that we need to be a little more specific. How do we get the wrong in students reversed without adding to it? Let me introduce three basic concepts.

Recall first that Christ turned the usual tactic of kingdom-building on its head. He entered history as a teacher, not as a warrior. Heart-centered correction likewise adheres to a teaching model for discipline rather than a manipulative or combative paradigm.

Before I explain this concept further, however, let's be clear on what it is not. Discipline through teaching does not denote sermonizing. Though a carefully worded monologue is sometimes appropriate, the model of discipline I suggest incorporates more than just lectures about the difference between right and wrong.

In a teaching model for discipline, the boundary between teaching and correction is not always distinguishable. For example, if the students aren't getting along with each other, a teacher might choose to employ an instructional strategy that encourages cooperation. I have used class-wide projects to build cohesiveness among students who would not accept each other. In working toward a common goal, the children set aside their differences and eventually began to see one another's gifts. That alternative teaching strategy, a class-wide project, helped to correct a problem that ordinarily would require a disciplinary measure.

On the other hand, while carrying out the process of discipline, a teacher may choose to instruct rather than punish. Not long ago our school custodian asked the teachers to address the boys of our grade about a mess they had created in their restroom. Even though imposing a consequence would have been entirely appropriate, we opted to first try talking with them instead. At recess we dismissed the girls and asked the guys to stay in their seats. Then we calmly described the unpleasant work that they had created for our janitor the previous day. "Disgusting," one of the boys remarked. We also noted that the person was not able to complete the task of cleaning their restroom until long after the students had gone home for the day. If the problem continued, we would have no choice but to allow only one student in the restroom at a time. After the boys assured us that they would change their behavior, we let them go. The "lesson" seemed to have hit its mark. Next afternoon the custodian told me that not only was the restroom much cleaner, it looked almost unused.

A teaching model for discipline helps students to see the natural consequences of their actions. One consequence of making a mess is having to clean it; the boys of our grade saw that someone else had unfairly "served" that consequence. The teaching framework for discipline may include the use of imposed consequences as well, but its real leverage is found not within the consequences themselves. Rather it draws strength from the classroom climate where correction occurs. Because students know that their teacher cares about them and about their learning, they are more willing to submit to that teacher's admonishment and to make changes when they are disciplined.

Second, recall again the wonderful paradox of Christ's kingdom, a realm that grows through self-sacrifice instead of through domination. Before connecting this idea to discipline, let me also clarify what sacrifice is not. Cross-bearing, as I said earlier, does not signify that believers have to atone for sin all over again. No, Christ's payment was sufficient for redeeming people from their sin. Nor does Christ's call to sacrifice oneself imply that teachers should let students do whatever they want; there is no restoration in allowing a wayward person to continue down the wrong path. How do we resolve the incongruity of prevailing over wrong by surrendering ourselves?

The apostle Paul settles it in Romans 12. Here he calls believers to offer their bodies as a living sacrifice, conforming no longer to the pattern of this world but following a new standard. One essential feature of the transformed life calls for treating one's enemies with kindness. Though the world's pattern is to *repay* evil for evil, Paul challenges believers to *overcome* evil with good. Repayment only continues a cycle of revenge. Those who seek to overcome wrong leave vengeance to God and work toward restoration, a process that almost always requires a sacrifice of some sort or another.

Heart-centered teachers become living sacrifices when they absorb the wrong that they receive from students, then offer back the thing those students *need* instead of what they *deserve*. In response to aloofness a teacher might offer kindness; in return for hostility a teacher would offer calmness. In dealing with student apathy, a teacher will work all the harder to make lessons meaningful. Some teachers even successfully use a sense of humor with kids who try to antagonize them. How do we hold students accountable for their actions when we soak up the wrong and offer good in return? As I have already said, imposed consequences are not absent from heart-centered classroom climate. Rather, teachers who allow students to face the consequences of their actions do so in a spirit of teaching rather than a spirit of retaliation.

Lastly, while a teaching model for discipline and a pattern of self-sacrifice results in far more success than a manipulative or vengeful pattern, this framework carries no guarantees for repairing wayward hearts; we cannot ultimately control the attitudes of our students. Before we get down on ourselves about this inability, though, let's think about the third concept, Christ's resurrection.

In raising Christ from the grave, God demonstrated his power over death and the curse of sin. The resurrection offers more than hope for what lies in eternity; it transforms lives today. Our God, who will one day resurrect dead bones, right now is also the One who softens and works new life into crusty, impenetrable hearts. Ultimately, Christ's Spirit must take care of the outlook overhaul. It is a freeing thought to realize that the final outcome of our work lies beyond our control. We don't need to stress ourselves when it looks like we aren't breaking through to students. We are permitted to live by what we hope for, and not just by what we see.

Conclusion

We have learned that our own attitudes as teachers can become an inhibiting factor when we address attitudes in students. Heart-centered teachers can break through this barrier by learning to see themselves and students within the context of the biblical narrative. One of the truths we find in this narrative is that God, the Creator of humans and hearts, is also the Redeemer. As followers of Christ, teachers of the heart will create conditions that allow for Christ-like attitudes to take root and grow, but Christ's Spirit must work the miracle of new life. This assurance allows us to operate in the gutsy mode of giving students what they need, not what they deserve. We move on now to look at the key components of a classroom climate that decreases resistance and nurtures a fresh outlook in students.

PART TWO:
HEART-CENTERED TEACHING

CHAPTER 4:
GETTING PERSONAL

Pressure

In the realm of do-it-yourself home repair projects, plumbing is the category that gives me the most frustration. That amazing creature called *water pressure*, domesticated to perform almost every kind of menial task from shower massage to the rinse cycle, is still a wild animal and will turn on you without a moment's hesitation if not securely confined.

A careless mistake can spell disaster, such as the time I failed to properly tighten a kitchen faucet several years ago during my first attempt at plumbing. I was on my way up the stairs after opening the main valve at the far end of the basement when I heard a gurgling noise. The loud "ker-lunk" and the roar which followed were the sounds of my faucet hitting the kitchen floor and a jet of water shooting straight up like a fire hose at my ceiling. Seconds ticked by like hours as I bounded over furniture and boxes to the far corner of a storage room where I had to fit a wrench to the main valve before turning the water off and stopping the geyser.

Most plumbing problems, thankfully, are not that dramatic. Still, at 40 pounds of pressure per square inch, even the smallest loose connection with water is unforgiving. The effects may be nearly imperceptible at first: a couple of tiny droplets on a cold pipe, dampness on the floor. By the next morning the moisture has become a puddle, and if the problem is not quickly addressed, the water will ruin the carpet and rot your floorboards.

In the world of plumbing, no factor is more crucial than a tight connection at every junction. The most elegant fixture is worthless without it. In a heart-centered classroom climate, *no condition is more important than positive relationships between the teacher and students.* Detailed lesson plans, glitzy technology, and flashy activities accomplish little if teachers and students do not get properly connected.

The effects of poor connections between teachers and students can be dramatic. Take, for instance, the child who starts arguments with the teacher during class or the group of students who laugh back as they are being reprimanded. Usually, though, the effects are more subtle. Students opt out of participating in discussion. They roll their eyes or mutter under their breath after discipline takes place. If the teacher-student relationship is not improved, the apathetic attitude can turn to animosity, ruining lessons and rotting out a motivation to learn.

It may be possible to manage a classroom without healthy connections between teachers and students. Manipulative teachers, who control with fear or who motivate with baskets of incentives, have little need for relationship building. A heart-centered climate, however, depends on the relationship factor. Now let's be clear. It is neither necessary nor healthy to have an intimate or chummy sort of relationship with each student. The goal is simply to earn the trust of students and understand them well enough to be able to respond to their needs. This understanding is essential both for meaningful teaching and for providing effective discipline, especially when attitude becomes a factor.

Unfortunately, positive relationships between teachers and students are commonly run off the rails by two distortions. In this chapter we examine these distortions and take a look at some ideas for building relationships in ways that escape their pull.

Overcoming Popularity Disorder

One of the biggest pitfalls to avoid in the area of building relationships is *popularity disorder*. This condition occurs when teachers become more concerned about what their students think of them than what they are trying to accomplish, when being highly thought of takes precedence to teaching in meaningful ways. Clinging to approval ratings, some teachers withhold discipline or look the other way when students misbehave. Popularity disorder can deter a teacher from setting high expectations or from pushing students to work to their potential. If teachers wish only to please their students, if they desire to be perceived as "cool" or "nice," they may be experiencing popularity disorder. While students might indeed use terms like cool or nice to describe their teacher who uses the heart-centered approach, seeking this kind of affirmation should not be part of that teacher's agenda.

For beginning teachers, being liked is often tied to a sense of survival. Over time, however, most of us recognize that relationships built on a need to be popular are superficial. They aren't real. Like water pipes sealed together with duct tape, those kinds of connections cannot withstand the pressure that often comes with learning and discipline.

A second outgrowth of popularity disorder is the tendency in teachers to compare themselves to other teachers. It bites when your students

like other teachers more than they like you, doesn't it? What do you do when it appears that you are second rate in their eyes? Of course it's never a bad idea to reflect on your practice, to look for areas where you could improve your teaching style or the way in which you interact with students. Student feedback should inform your practice, but it should never drive your practice. If you are making every effort to show kindness and to make learning meaningful, you have no need to worry about your students' relationships with other teachers. Teaching is not about you! It is not your job to be popular. Your calling as a teacher is to point to things greater than you, and to provide guidance where needed. The teaching profession depends on educators worthy of respect and trust; it does not rely on being the number-one adult in the lives of your kids. Affirmation certainly feels good, but it is only an occasional by-product of working with young people, and it is never guaranteed.

That second outgrowth of popularity disorder, the tendency to compare oneself to others, is a tough bug to exterminate. I was not able to get past it until I stopped focusing inwardly on my own personality and started to focus outwardly on my students. Taking a sincere interest in them (their learning and their lives), more than anything else, has been the key to conquering the popularity ailment. The practice of getting to know one's students, however, leads us to another problem that we must be on guard against.

Dodging the Labeling Distortion

Whereas the popularity disorder affects the way we view ourselves, labeling distorts the way we see our students. Without really thinking about it, we often categorize or pigeon-hole people in our minds, almost as if we were scientists and they were specimens. We group people according to their work or their interests, their possessions, or the friends with whom they associate. "Human taxonomies" can be useful, of course, in new surroundings. In joining a church, switching jobs, or moving to a new community, we use categories to make sense of who the people are. Categorizing becomes a distortion, though, when we use our systems to rate people or to assign them value. Furthermore, people taxonomies provide only a superficial sense of knowing others while we remain detached from them.

"Student classification," performed by teachers on their students, can also be a useful tool if its limits are kept in mind. At the beginning of a school year, for instance, it helps us get to know our students, and it helps us to find ways to meet their needs. We use classification to determine who needs extra help and who would benefit from enrichment, who should sit in the front of the room where their behavior can be monitored and who will be fine in less prominent places. As the year progresses we discover that some students are popular and that other students are not; that some are sports-minded or music-minded or computer-minded and so on. Student classification reveals certain things about who our students are; it helps to determine needs and uncover personality characteristics.

Classification is not generally a problem until teachers use classification to label or stereotype students. If we cement children into the categories our minds have created, our assumptions place limits on our teaching. It reduces what we can hope for or expect from the young people in our classrooms. For instance, if I cannot see beyond Tessa's chattiness or Jeremiah's reluctance to participate, I limit both my faith and my work. First, my attitude about Tessa and Jeremiah would constrict my trust in what the Holy Spirit can accomplish. Second, I'd be less than likely to work for growth in them or celebrate any progress that did occur. Though sorting students provides some useful knowledge, alone it achieves little in the work of teaching minds and hearts.[1]

Do you remember the story about the painter who came to my room before I started teaching? I couldn't put his wisdom to use because

---

1   To protect identities, I have changed the names of actual students in this book.

I did not see his son as an individual, as a person. After a week of interacting with him, my brain had labeled the young man as "naughty," and I could not imagine him in any other light. If I could have seen the person beneath the behavior, there would have been more to love and less to fear, more joy in the teaching and less stress in the correcting.

The labeling distortion perpetuates a distance between teachers and students and restrains heart-centered teaching and discipline. It's difficult to motivate students to learn, for example, if I haven't taken the time to discover what piques their interest. Providing meaningful correction is tough if I can't identify anything good in a person or if I haven't cared enough to find out why he might act the way he does. Part of heart-centered discipline consists of pointing to the unique ways the image of God is revealed in that individual's qualities. Discipline in this way provides a vision or a goal to aspire to rather than just reminding students of their failures.

Catching sight of the image of God in people also makes it easier to have faith in what God can accomplish, and seeing with the eyes of faith in turn improves my demeanor around students who are otherwise difficult to be around. Though I grew weary of prodding Miguel to complete his assignments, for example, his innate knowledge of animals always amazed me. Once when I stood scratching my head over where to search for our class's pet corn snake, which had disappeared from its cage, Miguel walked into the room and pulled it out from under a pillow in the corner. "I just knew it would want to hide there," he said when I asked him how he had found it so quickly. Another student, Casey, used to get on my nerves when she didn't pay attention in class, but somehow her witty sense of humor always pulled me out of the dumps on stressful days. Taking a person's redeeming qualities into account helps a teacher to see possibilities along with the faults and makes the discipline process a little less exasperating.

Finally, the labeling distortion can also build walls of resentment. I've had people assume things about me because of my occupation, my size, and my age. Thankfully, those experiences have been rare, but the wounds are still sensitive when they come to mind. The adjective "unassuming" describes a person who behaves humbly or without arrogance. In light of the labeling distortion, "unassuming" might also typify a teacher who is careful not to assume things of people because of their gender, how they look, who their friends are, or where their interests lie. By building connections, unassuming teachers learn to see students as "originals," masterfully crafted by God. The shortcomings each one deals with and the combination of hidden gifts each one possesses are all unique to the individual. Teachers who learn to view their students as persons are better equipped in making connections that are sincere.

How does a teacher move beyond the classification distortion and begin to see students as individuals, as persons? How does a person build positive relationships while avoiding the popularity disorder? Let's look at some ideas together.

Making Meaningful Connections

Making meaningful connections sometimes requires a new point of view, seeing yourself and your students with new eyes. Each of us has certain qualities that set us apart from others. In the classroom I can make difficult concepts clear. I can tell some pretty good stories and draw pictures that make students laugh. It's easy for me to find common ground in conversations with people because I've been to a lot of places and I've tried a lot of different things.

My humanity, though, also limits me. I am not the best at everything. For instance, I don't keep up with the shows young people watch or the music they listen to. I don't really follow any sports teams. In a crowd I am not going to be the center of attention. Students seem to respect me, but if they are looking for fun, I am not the first adult they seek out. Do I ever wish that I could do more or be more? Sometimes I do. Yet one blessing of growing older is recognizing that I can't be everything to everyone. I am grateful that God has created other adults to fill those roles with students that I cannot fill.

Being human also means that I am fallen. Often, the first thoughts that flip onto the screen in my brain when I wake up in the morning are replays of my recent blunders. The videos show students that I brushed off, decisions that were unfair or unwise, tasks uncompleted. If it were not for the grace of God, I'd be tempted to give up on my job and just stay in bed all day. The reality of grace restores my dignity so that I can apologize when I need to without condemning myself. Grace empowers me to forgive and mend relationships with students who have wronged me. Finally, it helps me to take myself a little less seriously and laugh at myself a little more. Seeing myself as a human, with unique qualities and shortcomings, is one side of making meaningful connections. The other side, of course, relates to the way we view our students.

Several years ago, when these ideas regarding classroom climate were forming in my mind, I committed myself to making time for paying attention to the students in my classroom. I decided that by the time they came to school in the morning, I would be finished with my preparations. I would stand by the door to greet them as they arrived and listen to their comments and stories. If no one came to talk to me, I would use the time to study them as they milled about, getting their things ready for the day.

I made the same commitment for lunch time and periodic recess times. I sat with students as they ate, talking with them if they included me and simply listening in on their conversations if they did not. At least once per week I asked to join in the games that they played at recess, though it wasn't long before they started to invite me.

The change I saw happening in me and in the students made it worth continuing the effort. As I became less concerned about having the right kind of personality and focused more on the people in my classroom, the students seemed to enjoy being around me more. Through my interacting with them outside of class, I remained the teacher but was somehow more human than the teacher they had known before. My perceptions of them also began to transform. No longer did they fit neatly into categories of obedient or naughty, gifted, average, or remedial. Instead they emerged from their pigeonholes and became living, breathing *original* people.

Getting connected lessened the barriers between us and increased the trust. They were more open in conversation and generally more receptive to my discipline. Though providing correction was still work, it was less taxing on my nerves because I understood more about why my students acted the way they did. One change I did not expect was how playing with my students outside would affect my attitude toward difficult students and my work with them. The adrenaline released in an active game is a huge stress reliever when things are not going well in the classroom. The diversion and the exertion of playing together releases the bad air and almost immediately changes the dynamics back inside the classroom.

At the same time I made the commitment to involve myself in the lives of the students, our school was also in the process of moving sixth grade away from a departmentalized setting toward a setting that was more self-contained. I resisted the change at first, thinking of all the work that was involved in doubling my subject preparation. I had no idea how the self-contained classroom would transform my view of learners or improve the quality of my teaching as a result.

Teachers in departmentalized settings will generally find it more difficult to build relationships, though there are people who do it well despite their situations. What is the key to getting connected if several classes of students pass through your room each day? How do teachers of older students work on relationships if students do not invite them into their conversations or to play games with them at recess? One way is to structure your learning activities at the beginning of a new school year in ways that allow you to get to know your students. Inviting their input on classroom rules or procedures is another way to learn about your students and to gain their trust. Attending students' events or asking about them is a way to demonstrate interest in their lives.

Those things considered, teachers of older students have said that connecting with students depends more on what a teacher *is* than on what a teacher *does*. Sincerity is fundamental in working with young people, and students have an uncanny way of detecting it. When you ask a question, your demeanor shows whether or not you really care about the answer. They know if you enjoy being around them or if your conversation is forced. They can tell if it's yourself that you are presenting or the kind of person you wish you were. They don't want to know every detail about your shortcomings, yet neither do they want you to act as if you had none. They also want you to be knowledgeable and passionate about your subject area. Ultimately, older students are not terribly different from the sixth graders that I work with. Students relate best to someone who is real, someone who is human.

My commitment to stay connected to the lives of my students, to show my humanity and to look for theirs, has made sincere relationships attainable. I should add, though, that perfect execution on all of these suggestions is neither possible nor necessary. Unforeseen problems occur, and I need the final ten minutes before school starts to get something ready for the day. After a bad morning I might feel too grumpy to sit with the students at lunch. Outside, the shade of the ash tree is sometimes just more inviting than a ball game in the hot sun. And an unexpected treat in the teacher's workroom almost always trumps chatting with students during break time!

Spending every free moment with students is not possible because I am human. Neither is it necessary because connecting with students is not a goal that is sought after for its own sake. It is through building relationships that the higher goals of heart-centered learning may be reached; therefore the habit of making oneself available to students is more important than strict adherence to a rule.

It has been a relief to find, through paying attention and being sincere, that I don't have to be someone I'm not. I don't have to change my life or personality or looks in order to meet my students' approval. As long as they know that I care about them and that they can trust me, I can live as the person I've been created to be and get on with the task I have been called to do.

Tough Nuggets

In a heart-centered classroom, it is worth the effort to develop positive relationships. Despite our best efforts, though, some young people are difficult to connect with. Perhaps you have students who do not care for you. Personalities clash, or you just don't have much in common with them. They've bonded with the person who teaches another subject or with the teacher they had the year before, but they choose to remain distant from you. Maybe they can't forgive you for something you once said or did. Or, you've been misrepresented by others who talked about you, and your students focus on that image instead of on the actual person that you are. You can gain some inroads with students like these, but you may never reach a point where you feel that you've bonded. They are tough nuts to crack.

My advice does not guarantee success; we're working with attitudes, after all. The first thing to remember, though, is that students aren't nuts! Most will not just split open and let you inside. Connecting with difficult students is a process. Moving closer to the goal, even if you never reach it, is better than giving up and remaining at odds with them.

Remember that students, regardless of personality, are generally more receptive to connecting with adults who treat them as persons, as original works of the divine Creator. Work at finding the unique goodness that God designed into each student. Point to it, and interact or teach in ways that bring it out.[2] Then try to see life the way they see it. No, you won't always agree with their feelings or their opinions, but if you knock down anyone who disagrees with you, don't expect seeing any changes in attitude. Finally, treat them as persons when you address the wrong. If you have already begun to discover the good in them, and if you have tried to see the world as they do, you'll reduce the risk of breaking connections in the discipline you provide, no matter how painful the correction needs to be. Gaining students' *trust* is more important than scoring admiration. If you can get a student to trust you, your ability to provide heart-centered teaching and discipline will be much higher, even perhaps than those teachers who desire to be popular.

---

2   John Van Dyk calls this process "unfolding." Van Dyk, J. (2005). *The craft of Christian teaching*. Sioux Center, Iowa: Dordt Press.

If students still show no signs of coming around, I'd suggest that you continue to honor and affirm them as image bearers of God, regardless of their lack of acceptance for you. Though we can often change behavior through coercion, we can only invite or encourage a change in attitude. Our ultimate calling, as followers of Christ, is to love the way Christ loved, without counting the costs or checking for a return on the "investment."

Treating students as humans touches on the somewhat controversial topic of self-esteem. We should examine this subject for a few moments before we close this chapter.

Self-Esteem and Attitude

The way we interact with our students greatly affects the way our students perceive themselves. Moreover, when students feel accepted by the teacher, the goals of the heart-centered classroom are far more attainable than when students do not feel accepted.

Though self-esteem is a familiar topic in education, it is not always a popular one. Sometimes sparks fly at the mention of it. I will never forget the seasoned teacher who shared her views during one of my first workshops on classroom management and discipline. She had been teaching high schoolers longer than I had been alive. Her baritone voice had gone scratchy from years of smoking, and she punctuated most of her opinions with a swear word or two. "I have a curriculum to get through," she snorted, "and you're telling me I gotta help my kids *feel good* about themselves?"

If helping students to "*feel good* about themselves" becomes the chief goal, her point is legitimate. The practical problems with self-esteem are not difficult to see. First, there is the issue of honesty. Teachers wanting children to always have high opinions of themselves have to praise everything, whether it is worthy of praise or not. Furthermore, because telling a person they have done wrong doesn't exactly skyrocket them to the top of the self-esteem chart, corrective discipline becomes a problem too. Finally, the question of using time responsibly enters in, as the woman in my workshop pointed out, if classroom activities have more to do with boosting egos than with learning.

Beyond the pragmatic problems, self-esteem is also seen by some as a spiritual problem. The focus, it seems, should be on others and God, rather than on one's "self." John Piper of Desiring God Ministries argues that self-esteem deprives people of a sense of the glory of God. It's pretty difficult to build self-esteem in someone and point to God's greatness at the same time, notes Piper. People don't travel to the Grand Canyon, for example, to stand and gaze at themselves in a mirror. "Making much" of someone is not what God's love is about. Loving another is doing what is best for that person. Love points others to God and to the truth.[3]

Loving God and others are fundamental commandments in scripture, of course. Narcissism, conceit, and arrogance turn love inward and should be avoided. Yet I would argue that self-esteem is a prerequisite for helping people to look outward. Personal experience gives evidence to this belief. As I said earlier, I've felt the sting of stereotyping, and I have been judged as a person because of mistakes or misrepresentation. In those situations, the hurt turned my focus *in* to the self and away from the task at hand or the good of the people around me. All that mattered to me was preserving myself, trying to prove something about myself, or even removing myself from the situation. When we are misunderstood or treated with indifference, we have difficulty looking beyond ourselves to work that needs doing or to the needs of others. We might also be reluctant in those situations to confess wrongdoing because we are too concerned with protecting ourselves. If our feelings or our sense of self-worth is tromped on, it's interesting how much more important that *self* becomes for us. This discussion leads us to a paradox: self-preservation and self-centeredness, the negative stuff usually associated with self-esteem, is actually heightened when a person's self-esteem is ignored.

As followers of Christ, we could take some cues from the life of Christ in this issue. While he left us with no explicit instructions on self-esteem, Jesus did make a habit out of assigning value to people who had none. He saw the good, or at least the potential, in folks known to be hussies and fraudsters. His kindness seemed to be more effective at changing lives than the reproach of society was.

If we associate self-esteem with a confidence in one's own worth and abilities, then self-esteem is not the problem. A healthy amount of it is what gives us the courage to break free of ourselves, to admit our mistakes, to ask questions, and to take risks. Self-esteem is essential for venturing out to help someone in need or for considering someone else's point of view before making up one's mind. For all of the difficult things we and our students need to do, self-esteem is a necessity.

How can we help students to know they have worth so that they can see beyond themselves? While highlighting the value in persons partly involves the things we say directly, such as our compliments or praise, in building relationships affirming the good is more about the way we

---

3   Piper, J. (2007). *Don't waste your life*. Wheaton, Illinois: Crossway Books.

show it. The ideas that I have already mentioned—taking an interest in the lives of students, listening when they talk, making time to play with them, laughing at the funny things they say, smiling at their quirks—all of these acts of love build self-acceptance or self-esteem.

How does self-esteem enter in when contriteness of heart is key to a change of heart? This is a question that merits more consideration than space allows here. We will take it up in Chapter Ten on making personal confrontations.

Conclusion

Maintaining positive relationships moves our influence beyond a need for coercion to a position of affecting the way our students perceive the world, how they feel about it, and how they respond. Teachers of the heart build connections by seeing themselves as persons and by treating their students as persons. Having examined the topic of teacher-student relationships, let's move on to explore the way students relate to each other in a heart-centered classroom climate.

CHAPTER 5:
CULTIVATING COMMUNITY

Tomatoes Versus Thistles

Fresh, home-grown vegetables taste better than mass-produced, store-bought ones. For that reason, each year I try my hand at gardening when spring finally relocates to our part of the globe. It's invigorating to dig in the dirt and scatter a few seeds. Even watering is something I have grown to enjoy—when I get around to it. My trouble is that gardening never produces immediate results. A couple of weeks after planting, I lose heart when there still isn't any produce to eat!

Growing new attitudes in students also requires perseverance. Gardening is a pretty good analogy to enlist as we cultivate community in the classroom. Let's briefly look at a few other aspects of gardening that will serve as parallels to developing community.

In gardening, the absence of weeds does not translate into the presence of a crop. You can hack at thistles until the soil is bare, but they'll grow back before your eyes if you don't fill the space with something else. Cultivating actual vegetables keeps weeds in check. Whereas daffodils and broccoli won't totally snuff out their unwelcome competitors, a healthy crop of desirable plants does make it harder for the annoying stuff to get cozy.

So gardeners plant seeds and make sure that those seeds can feel the sun, a must for germination and photosynthesis. Still, planting seeds is not the essence of gardening any more than clearing weeds is. The vegetables have to be cultivated: someone must tend to their needs. People who have patience for this part of the process do certain things that their plants like, and their plants return the favor by giving them food.

For the first time a few summers ago, I grew some tomatoes and made salsa. My wife gets credit for watering them, and Stan, a retired farmer who lives down the street, should be acknowledged for the advice he shared on fertilizing: "*Llama beans*, Al. You've gotta throw some llama beans in the hole before you stick the tomatoes in the ground. Gives em a good boost." It took me a week to realize that he was talking about animal dung and not the things people add to chili.

When I tasted the first fresh tomato, however—the fruit of that puny sprout I had cupped in my hand three months before—I realized that even with my investment of time and energy, the whole phenomenon of producing fruit is still a miracle. Thanks be to God!

As with gardening, I often find it difficult to persevere in cultivating a spirit of community in the classroom. The reason it's such a headbanger is that no matter what seeds I plant, I can't control what my students do to each other. Rules and consequences help, of course. I can hold students accountable for what I see, but dealing with the problems that occur behind my back is a lot trickier. Children can be mean to each other. How can we get students to show kindness, to respect one other? How can we get the harvest of true community?

Clearing Weeds and Planting Seeds

In reaction to school violence, schools often adopt "zero-tolerance" policies or other kinds of systems to keep harassment in check. Students have a right to feel safe; schools and classrooms need rules and consequences to protect children and to hold bullies accountable. In the same vein, school-wide respect policies often focus on words and behaviors that will not be allowed: putdowns, name-calling, harassment, and so on. The absence of harassment, however, does not translate into the presence of kindness. A climate-controlled classroom works hard to keep the outward forms of harassment at bay, but it does not stop there. Heart-centered teachers realize that policies and programs cannot be successful unless the classroom climate is also addressed. We have to deal with the attitudes that give rise to harassment, and we need to grow something in their place.

Near the beginning of a new school year, teachers will often "plant the seeds" of community with mixers to help their students get to know each another. They may also use team-building exercises that require their students to cooperate in order to accomplish a mutual goal. These sorts of activities effectively grow necessary classroom skills like listening and encouraging. In addition, teachers sometimes set aside time during devotions or announcements to review the meaning of living and working in community.

As vital as talk about community and team-building activities are, however, they do not make up the essence of living in harmony, just as planting seeds is not the sum and substance of growing tomatoes. Replacing egocentric or discourteous tendencies with respect calls for more than just activities or discussions.

Before we consider ways to encourage respect, perhaps we should think about what constitutes "respect." Interestingly, the term derives from the Latin word *spicere*, which means "look at, or see." I like that connection! Though showing respect has much to do with behaviors and words that we avoid, the act of respecting is also about the way we view each other. Once again, it's about attitude. In a heart-centered classroom, one of the goals is for students to *see* each other as worthy persons and to treat each other as such.

Because fostering respect encompasses more than merely eliminating harassment, this chapter is not going to address the outward forms of unkindness that make their presence known at school. Also, because I'd suspect that most of us could find lessons or activities on respecting our classmates, we aren't going to spend time on "planting seeds" here either. Instead, we will look at *cultivating*, the day-to-day work that it takes to foster an attitude of respect and a spirit of cooperation in the classroom.

Honoring the Difference
If we think about respect as an attitude that we strive to grow, we should be aware of two weeds that compete with respect: prejudice and envy. Let's get the lowdown on these invaders and explore some strategies for limiting their presence in the classroom.

Prejudice
Prejudice inhibits our ability to see good in others who are not like us. A key for dismantling prejudice among students is to first examine our own attitudes and then model the attitudes that we desire in the students. How do we view those whose personalities or abilities differ from our own? What do we think of young people who come to us from different family situations or cultures? How do we respond to students who need extra help or who push the lines of discipline?

Teachers who cultivate community believe that each individual comes to the group with something unique to offer—especially those who appear or act different from the rest—and they look for those God-given qualities as they get to know each student. It might be a keenness for detail or a knack for recalling random facts. Some have the ability to lead; others demonstrate the gift of listening. Certain students work with neatness or keep things organized, while others find creative solutions to problems that arise. In addition to special abilities, the different members of a classroom also come with unique perspectives. Students of different nationalities may help to broaden an understanding of culture and people. Learners whose views on politics or justice differ from the majority of their classmates can enrich classroom discussions. Finally, students who see humor in ordinary situations often liven things up with their comments or put people on the same level with the laughter they generate.

As teachers discover—or uncover—the distinctive combination of gifts and perspectives in students, they find ways to highlight those features or put them to use. A teacher may point out the benefits of growing up bilingual or create opportunities for students to talk about their family traditions. If a student's unconventional point of view triggers sneers or whispers, a teacher might reveal a kernel of truth in that perspective that others have missed. An English teacher I know goes out of her way to include the voices of all class members. After seeking permission, she shares insights that different students have written, choosing selections both from those who express their thoughts readily in class and from those who tend to remain quiet. A science teacher at our school likes to recognize the diversity of abilities by including alternatives for assessment. Students may occasionally opt out of traditional written tests, for example, by constructing products that demonstrate knowledge of the content standards.

In addition to honoring different abilities and different perspectives, teachers also need to monitor their attitudes toward children who cause trouble. Students often presume that teachers dislike mischief-makers, but they will not sense that unfriendliness in teachers who deliberately cultivate community. Students need to be held accountable for their actions, of course, but heart-centered teachers do not carry grudges. After addressing misdeeds, a teacher may draw wayward students back into classroom discussions or look for positive behaviors to acknowledge. Outside of class, a person can banter with mischievous and compliant children alike. Teachers who consistently demonstrate indestructible love for students model another important truth about respect: we are called to value not only those who have different interests or abilities, but also those who occasionally displease us.

Envy

A habit of accentuating the positive in all students keeps prejudice at bay and encourages respect. A common relative of prejudice, though, is envy. Whereas prejudice fails to see the good in others, envy recognizes what others have and feels resentment. Those who envy suffer a disgruntled longing for the things or the qualities that others possess.

Teachers give rise to envy in the classroom when they show favoritism. Even though no caring teacher would knowingly demonstrate partiality, children are sensitive to issues of fairness. They notice when certain students are chosen for special privileges or roles more often than others. Of course some teachers will point out that life isn't fair and that sensitive kids should learn to deal with disappointments. I would argue that authentic Christian communities demonstrate a more desirable way of living and working together rather than simply mimicking the practices of people who care only for themselves. Teachers who cultivate community show impartiality for a bigger reason than the avoidance of misgivings among students, then. Their dedication to fairness teaches students that every person has worth. In an effort to minimize envy when privileges or roles are assigned, teachers often create systems of taking turns so that all students are offered an opportunity. A container with names on cards or Popsicle sticks is an easy way to insure that students are chosen at random when participation or help is needed.

Fairness does not mean that all students receive equal treatment, of course. When it comes to certain roles in the classroom, some children are better equipped to serve than others. Not everyone possesses the ability to lead a small group, for example. If a certain skill is vital in carrying out a particular task, a teacher needs to be transparent and explain the reasons behind his or her choices. In a recent small group activity, where students practiced the tedious skill of documenting sources for research, I told the class that our six leaders for the exercise were those who had already demonstrated competence in the task. The members in each group would need to rely on their leaders for answering questions and for checking the accuracy of their work.

The reality that "fair is not equal" also applies in situations where students receive extra help. If a student asks why the learning is modified for some or why certain classmates get to work with the teacher or paraprofessional in a small group, a person would truthfully explain that the extra help is based on need.

In summary, respect has much to do with honoring differences. Teachers can curb prejudice and envy, the two enemies of respect, by valuing diversity and resisting favoritism. Teaching students to respect each other is fundamental: a community cannot survive unless individuals honor one another. However, there is more to a thriving classroom community than respect alone.

Making a Difference
Another attitude we strive for in building community is the servant

heart. A heart of service values others above self, looking not only to its own interests but also to the interests of others.[4] It finds meaning not by boosting one's own status but instead through making a difference in someone else's life. Let's examine a couple of areas where teachers can encourage students to focus on the needs of the people around them.

Opportunities to Serve

One way of encouraging servant hearts is through providing opportunities to serve. Busy classrooms generate many tasks that require attention: materials must be set out or handed out, work areas have to be tidied, and certain teaching demonstrations require assistance. Teachers may ask for help with these needs as they arise or divvy them up and ask different students to take charge of them for periods of time.[5]

Regardless of the method, the key to encouraging a heart of service is inviting students to give of themselves rather than enticing their assistance through external forms of motivation. Teachers who feel obligated to "pay" children for their service inadvertently misdirect their students' focus. Instead of concentrating on the needs of others, students wind up thinking about what they stand to gain. Also, as I said in Chapter Two, rewarding children for completing classroom tasks often leads to envy or resentment. As a result, the practice usually dismantles community instead of building it up. Even though rewards may encourage the *actions* of service, they do not always foster an *attitude* of service.

What is the best way to respond, then, when students give of their time to help with tasks in the classroom? An essential ingredient of motivation, obviously, is tapping into the power of positive feedback. Compliments boost our self-confidence and motivate us to do our best. All of us occasionally need someone to notice our abilities or the efforts we have made. Praise offered with sincerity is a great source of encouragement:

"Your leadership in our activity was excellent."

"Hey, nice work on organizing those bookshelves."

In terms of growing servant hearts, though, we also want to look for ways to demonstrate that the work of students benefits the people around them. If community is valued, the real reward in serving is knowing that one's effort benefited the community, that the service made a difference.

---

4   Philippians 2:3-4.

5   Some of the monthly roles in my classroom include technical support, postal service, lunch-card dispenser, librarian, duster, and seating official. The person who assigns seats has the challenge of pairing each student with someone that they have not sat next to before. In addition, I reserve the right to make changes before the desks are moved.

Teachers can highlight the effect of service on the community through feedback that is more specific than a general *nice work* or *good job*:

"I really appreciated the way that you kept your team on track today."

"Thanks for your help in the reading corner. It's going to be a lot easier for us to find our books now."[6]

Perhaps you noticed that both of those examples included an expression of gratefulness as well. Similar to external rewards, you see, compliments acknowledge the actions of serving, but gratitude highlights the attitude. Let me explain it this way. With adequate resources, we can obtain almost any service we desire, from attention in a restaurant to car care. However, there is no fee that will procure a *spirit* of service, such as kindness, compassion, or neighborliness. Those dispositions are matters of the heart. They cannot be extracted; they can only be given. Therefore, a sincere expression of thanks is often the most appropriate response to a person's contribution.[7]

Room for Humor
Creating a heart-centered classroom climate consumes a great deal of energy. Heart-centered teachers work to build positive relationships with students who sometimes resist them, for instance. They motivate and encourage others, even when they themselves feel down. As we will see later, teachers may also be called to override their feelings of anger or frustration in the discipline they provide. Making room for laughter is one way that teachers can allow students the opportunity of contributing to a positive classroom atmosphere instead of managing all of the work on their own.

Any quick-witted teacher can use humor to lighten the mood, but effective teachers also skillfully use the jests and banter of students to boost morale. Adults who enjoy working with young people know that students can exhibit a wonderful sense of humor. Why not capitalize on it?

---

6   Teachers need to exercise sensitivity about the feedback that they give, of course. Even though public acknowledgment helps students to see the good in their classmates, it can also lead to envy or self-centeredness. For that reason, teachers should avoid ranking children in their feedback. In addition, older students may feel embarrassed when people recognize their abilities in front of others. Sensitive teachers take the personalities of their students into account when they express their approval.

7   In some cases, a compliment in response to a gift may be perceived as an insult; it assesses the value of the gift and thereby cheapens its worth. Sincere appreciation, on the other hand, acknowledges that the value of the gift is immeasurable, that the recipient is indebted to the giver.

Some children are gifted at making funny remarks that cause us to see things with a new perspective. Thinking of an example to share is difficult, unfortunately, because most of those comments seem humorous only within the context in which they are made. Other children help us to laugh at ourselves. My students make fun of my work car, for example, a 1950's model suburban that was once used to transport school children. Between the spots of rust, you can still see its original bus-yellow paint-job. Kids also crack jokes about my chicken-scratch handwriting and my absent-minded mistakes.

I welcome good-natured jokes directed at me not only because I enjoy laughing at myself but also because it seems to help uptight students to take their own weaknesses a little less seriously. Part of our ability to respect others arises out of first finding the grace to accept ourselves.

Certain kinds of laughter, of course, are intolerable in a heart-centered classroom. I get grumpy when students laugh about things behind my back or when the subject of humor detracts attention from learning. Neither can I permit joking that makes others feel small. Overall, though, submitting occasionally to the urge to laugh shows children that their presence makes a positive difference in the classroom.

Unfortunately, the dynamics of a group do not always allow for uplifting humor. Negative children spoil it by scorning the clever remarks of others. Teachers who lack rapport among a group see their zingers ricochet off the stone faces of their students. These kinds of situations are unfortunate, of course. Teaching is much more fun when students enjoy each other, when they bond. Still, teachers should not fret when they can't create that kind of atmosphere. Even though camaraderie makes for a fun teaching environment, the formation of friendships is not something a teacher can really control—and neither should it be our goal. Authentic communities, you see, are built on more than just positive relationships.

Getting It to Grow
So far we have talked about teaching students to respect each other. We have also explored strategies for encouraging students to contribute to the community in positive ways, to make a difference in the lives of others. However, we still have one key ingredient of community to explore.

Living communities are like vines. They thrive when they connect to something outside of themselves. All around us we see communities that grow around work, recreation, or interests. Parents chat with each other about their kids at sporting events. Teachers laugh and commiserate over food in the faculty lounge. Farmers talk about weather and livestock prices at the sale barn. Churches form around a common love for the Lord and common ways of expressing beliefs. When people come together through a purpose that is larger than themselves, community becomes organic. It has life.[8]

At school, learning and the learning tasks ought to be the central thing, the foundation for community. We need to work at connecting young people not just with each other but with their learning. Teachers striving for a *learning* community design learning experiences that propel students beyond themselves. They point at the problem to be solved, the mystery to be unraveled, the beauty to be enjoyed.[9] Of course, getting young people to concentrate on anything outside of themselves is no small challenge. However, if a teacher is able to draw students in to the topic at hand, the interchange that takes place fosters a more authentic sense of community, like those that grow naturally outside the walls of the classroom. We will look more closely at the issue of capturing interest in the next chapter.

The matter I would like to explore here relates to building a spirit of cooperation. How can we encourage students to work together, to support each other in their learning? Let's look at a few strategies.

Structured Cooperation

Cooperative learning has often proven itself effective in connecting students with each other and their studies. Over the years, I have seen many children develop greater tolerance for their classmates and become more engaged in a topic as a result of learning in cooperation.

Unfortunately, the term cooperative learning is frequently misunderstood and misapplied. In his book, *The Craft of Christian Teaching*, education professor John Van Dyk notes that teachers often substitute cooperative learning with a process he has labeled as "simply group work."[10] When a teacher assigns students to engage in small group activities without any instructions about individual responsibilities within each group, that method is simply group work. Though simply group work may look like cooperative learning on the surface, genuine cooperation is rare. Typically one or two motivated students within each group do most of the work, while the others mess around or just tune out.

One particularly harmful variety of simply group work is assign-

---

8   Lief, J. (2010). [Personal conversation with Jason Lief].

9   Palmer, P. J. (2007). *The courage to teach: Exploring the inner landscape of a teacher's life.* San Francisco: Jossey-Bass.

10 Van Dyk, J. (2005). *The craft of Christian teaching.* Sioux Center, Iowa: Dordt Press.

ing a group activity and then asking students to form their own groups. Socially confident students love this kind of freedom, of course. In my early years, their approval was one of my greatest reasons for allowing it. "*Thanks,* Mr. B!" It was an ingenious strategy, I thought. By allowing children to choose their teams, I saved myself the work and made students happy as well. The unwelcome repercussions of the strategy are less noticeable; for example, shy children usually keep their anxieties hidden. Through my experience as a parent, I have learned that some students worry a great deal about situations where students choose their groups. In addition, the rejection they sometimes encounter in those predicaments further undermines their self-confidence. Teachers who wish to build community remove the potential for anxiety and rejection with appropriate amounts of structure.

In planning for a successful cooperative learning experience, teachers strive for two goals. First, as the word "learning" suggests, students need to acquire knowledge or skills through the activity. If the assignment does not help the students to learn something as well as—or more deeply than—they could learn it through direct instruction, then the effort is not worth the time. Therefore, every cooperative learning exercise is carefully planned and monitored in order to insure that the activity is meaningful—that the learning objective is met.

Second, as the descriptor "cooperative" suggests, each member has a task to perform. No group can accomplish its work adequately without the positive involvement of everyone. In most learning settings, sincere cooperation requires some explicit instruction on the skills of cooperation and perhaps some modeling or role play. Occasionally, before starting an activity, I invite a few students to sit in a circle in the front of the classroom and pantomime "non-listening" behaviors, then "listening" behaviors for the rest of the class. Some kids naturally love to ham it up in those impromptu performances, making the demonstration not only meaningful but fun. After a few laughs and a short discussion on the actions observed, students begin their learning task with a clear picture of not just the learning goal but also the manner of behaving that the small-group setting requires.

Cooperative learning is also more effective when the teacher and students evaluate the process after the activity is completed. Evaluation does not always require a formal process where everyone fills out a form, for example. Teachers can get students thinking about their "cooperative progress" by simply noting specific things that seemed to go better this time than the time before or by pointing out some of the snags that developed and asking students to suggest how those problems could be avoided in future activities. Often, students have their own ideas about improvement.

When structured cooperation is carefully planned, and when teachers take time to reflect with students on the goals and outcomes of the strategy, cooperative learning enhances learning and cultivates community.

Unprompted Cooperation

Sincere cooperation in a heart-centered classroom is not necessarily limited to specific activities crafted by the teacher. Teachers also cultivate the spirit of a learning community when they allow, or even encourage, students to seek each others' help on challenging tasks.

In the 1920s and early 1930s, psychologist Lev Vygotsky investigated the tendency in both adults and children to verbalize their way through new undertakings and difficult problems. Talking aloud seems to help the mind process unfamiliar information. His work has influenced some of the current research on collaboration, a topic we will visit in greater depth next chapter. This inclination to talk while solving a problem is worth noting here, though. Some students learn more effectively when they are allowed to communicate with themselves or with others as they work.[11]

Knowing that certain students need to talk their way through difficult tasks, community-oriented teachers adapt their management style of work time and study halls to accommodate that learning style. Whereas they don't deny that children can be tempted to abuse the privilege of working with a peer, in reality, some students lack the confidence to attack a difficult problem on their own without someone near. Others lack the self-assurance to put words on a blank sheet of paper without first verbalizing their ideas with others. Accounting for the fact that unprompted collaboration offers temptations as well as benefits, teachers who are serious about keeping the focus on learning might reconsider the practice of using study times as "prep periods" for their own work. When students ask to sit together, a teacher who checks regularly on progress and offers an occasional word of encouragement or advice conveys the message that learning is expected. Coaching students on how to work with someone instead of doing the work for them helps to build the skills

---

11 Tinzmann, M. B., Jones, B. F., Fennimore, T. F., Bakker, Fine, J. C., & Pierce, J. (1990). *What is the collaborative classroom?* NCREL, Oak Brook, 1990. Retrieved February 20, 2011, from http://www.arp.sprnet.org/admin/supt/collab2.htm.

that make collaboration possible.

Not everyone agrees that allowing students to help each other during work time is a good idea. One criticism I hear occasionally is that allowing children to work with partners teaches them to become overly dependent on others. I have two responses to this argument.

The first one draws from interactions I see in the world outside of school, the world we are preparing our students to serve in eventually. Do business or factory employees practice new skills in total isolation? Rarely. What would be the sense of secluding a laborer from the watchful eyes of coworkers who could offer advice or prevent costly mistakes on a product? How often do engineers, doctors, mechanics, or lawyers solve difficult challenges without consulting other professionals who are familiar with the kinds of problems they are working on? Even though I am a fairly confident writer, I almost always consult others if the piece is for a public audience. Others assist me in the planning, the revising, and the editing of my work.

Yes, there is value in the personal struggle. None of us would improve at anything if we allowed someone else to do it for us. But cooperation is not about allowing one person in the relationship to do all of the work. It's about having a helper close by when someone cannot get any farther on his own. It's about students taking responsibility for their neighbors' learning. Obviously, I do not excel at every task that I undertake. Yet, I am willing to try things that are difficult if I can count on someone for advice. Thanks to the help of friends and neighbors, I now understand much more than I once did about certain tasks that used to give me a headache—like plumbing and gardening for instance!

My second response to the argument against unprompted cooperation draws from the results I have personally seen. Ironic perhaps, but working with someone else is the very thing that seems to help many students improve at working independently. Why? Success has much to do with building confidence. Students who struggle with new concepts develop a faith in their own ability when they work through new ideas with the encouragement, or even just the presence, of another individual.

Perhaps my best example from a recent year would be Jake, who began sixth grade with an aversion to math. As soon as something didn't make sense to him, he would shut down, and no amount of coaxing or threatening on my part could convince him to even try. Around Christmas time Daniel started to ask if he could sit with Jake during study hall. They would work through the assignments together, and because the two are good friends, math did not seem like such a chore to Jake. Daniel must have explained things in a way that made sense to Jake. Today Jake is often among the first to catch on in math lessons, and though he and Daniel still enjoy working together, he often completes assignments on his own.

This example is not isolated. Variations of it happen nearly every year. Fear or dislike for learning is gradually replaced by confidence and sometimes even enjoyment when students are permitted the support of a peer in difficult tasks. The opportunity also changes students' attitudes toward each other. Some grow a desire to encourage the struggling, and others grow in respect for the strengths of their classmates instead of envying or belittling them.

Conclusion

Communities are living entities that must be cultivated rather than coerced. Teachers can foster the attitudes of a thriving classroom community by teaching students to respect differences, by providing opportunities for them to make a positive difference in the classroom, and by encouraging cooperation.

There is too much to say about the important topic of community, though, in just one chapter. What about disagreements, for example? Should an "argument" always be seen as a threat to community, or could a healthy disagreement signify a deeper or more authentic form of respect? How do we work through problems that threaten a sense of community in a classroom? These topics will come up again as we look next at heart-centered teaching and later as we discuss corrective discipline in a heart-centered climate (Chapter Eleven).

CHAPTER 6:
CONFRONTING THE BEASTS

A Real Zoo

The Wilderness Kingdom Zoo was not well marked, and global positioning hadn't been invented yet. Finding that place in the hilly timber of Iowa's deep south demanded the cooperation of every navigator on board. My mom, who can only make sense of maps when she is headed north, was perched on her knees in the front seat, facing the rear of the car and calling out directions. The rest of us had our faces pressed up to the windows we had been assigned while we scanned fences and telephone poles in search of any marker that would lead us to the trail. My young nephew finally spotted the sign on our third pass down one stretch of highway. Hand-painted on a weathered barn board, it pointed to a one-lane gravel road that quickly disappeared in the trees.

Eventually we ended up on an old farm place, the home of the zoo. A woman, who had been revving the engine of an old Ford Galaxie while a man peered under the hood, noticed us and came to greet us. She led us inside a feed shed resting on cement blocks where she took our money. Another door on the opposite side of the shed happened to be the entrance to the zoo. Our then two-year-old daughter Samantha discovered this access when she leaned against the door and fell out, onto the back of a sleeping llama. Scared out of her wits, she screamed for a good five minutes after being rescued. The animal, however, unstartled by all of the commotion, continued to lie where it was, forcing the rest of us to jump over it to enter the zoo.

The familiar rules about safety which you may find constricting about other zoos were not a factor here. The animals at the Wilderness Kingdom Zoo were classified in two groups and housed accordingly. Those able to eat full-grown humans were securely locked within cages made of chicken wire, while all the others were free to roam about and attack the guests. These "less dangerous" animals included about everything you could think of: four-legged creatures from raccoons to deer and two-legged ones from chickens to emus.

Another element you may be accustomed to at traditional zoos are the little plaques with scientific names and other educational information. Nothing of the sort could be found here, and neither were the zoo keepers much help in answering questions. Everything we asked was met with a similar response: "Hmmm. Don't know."

"That furry thing sitting on the fence over there. What is that?"

"Don't know."

"Okay, those wolf pups my nephews are holding and petting right now, have they been vaccinated for rabies?"

"Hmmm. Couldn't tell ya."

Though the zoo keepers were frightfully uninformed about the animals in their care, I would not say that our visit to Wilderness Kingdom lacked that educational quality we like to provide for our children. The learning was just more experiential. For example, instead of reading on a sign about the way that each creature gives and takes within its habitat, at this zoo you actually get drawn into the ecological cycle, vying to preserve your own life while not becoming food for something else.

You see, the zoo keepers at Wilderness Kingdom provide food for their animals by way of a system that is both ingeniously simple and cost-efficient. They have the guests pay to do the feeding. This method generates more revenue for the zoo and frees up the zoo keepers to pursue other interests. Those not working on their cars, for example, found great amusement in leaning against the fence and watching the animals batter the visitors.

Half a dozen candy dispensers are located in various places around the zoo. When a quarter is turned into one of the machines, a mixture of bread and vegetables slides into a cup. What you should really do then is heave the food over your shoulder and run for your life. The animals, who could work a bit on self-control, get very pushy around anyone who is caught hoarding (which is what we were trying to do). Tossing food on the ground, after we'd paid for money for it, seemed wasteful. No, our intention was to hold onto our treats and dole them out at a sensible pace.

The longest any of the food cups stayed in our hands was about 10 seconds. A herd of goats took out my mom as she was making a break for the lamb pen. My sister, holding her cup high above her head, had been gaining distance on a group of sheep but went sprawling when a goose came out of nowhere and ran between her legs. My brother-in-law, who had been observant enough to wait until the goats and sheep were off pillaging someone else, involuntarily flung his food into the air when he got snuffed by a deer. "Snuffing," by the way, is when an animal inserts its nose under a person's backside and applies a quick upward thrust.

When we stopped buying food, the free-range animals finally left us alone, and we were able to take in some of the other exhibits. Though it would be fun for me to tell you more about the peculiarities of this menagerie, I would like to take you to another zoo. It is a place we visited later that same summer, and it was different from Wilderness Kingdom in about every way you could imagine. Situated in the city of Sioux Falls, the Great Plains Zoo takes pride in its neatness, safety, and educational focus. Gracefully curved concrete paths connect an array of fine cages. Educational markers inform guests of the taxonomy and natural habitats of animals safely locked behind bars or high fences. We were gladly able to let down our guard at this zoo as we walked with Samantha, who did not beg to be carried everywhere. Though not everyone takes time to study the information on little signs at zoos, that slightly annoying teacher aspect of my personality wants to read everything I see, and at the Great Plains Zoo, my appetite for knowledge found plenty of what it craved.

I honestly enjoyed our visit there. However, something significant seemed to be lacking when compared to our other zoo experience. At Great Plains we felt safe but disconnected, informed of the facts yet deprived of reality. Back at Wilderness Kingdom in southern Iowa, if the urge came over you, you could actually stick your hand through the wire of a cage and have it bitten off by a bear or a lion. It's not that I would have been foolish enough to try, but just having the option made our visit there more real, more authentic. At Great Plains we were separated from most of the larger animals by a double fence or a deep chasm dug into the ground which kept the creatures from getting too close to the guests, and to our disappointment, some animals were not even visible because of their distance from us.

There's an analogy in those two zoos that applies to the topic of classroom climate; the differences between them highlight a dilemma in the area of learning and its appeal to students. Disconnectedness between students and their learning, or between students and the learning process, creates barriers that impede motivation. Finding safe ways to minimize these barriers is another key to creating a heart-centered classroom climate.

Barriers to Learning

Student apathy toward learning is a major source of frustration for teachers. For one, discipline problems usually escalate when kids don't want to learn. Worse, when students regularly tune out or complain about the teacher's instruction, that person may wonder if he has grown incompetent or irrelevant. To offset indifference in the classroom, teachers commonly provide diversions, such as rewarding students for hard work or adding games "to make learning fun." While the diversion strategy may remove the obstacle temporarily, it can also perpetuate the notion that learning itself is dull and unpleasant.

Apathy among students is frequently the result of factors outside of school and outside of our control. Yet the way students often experience learning at school also creates a barrier. In many classrooms, learners are kept at a safe distance from the things they are learning. School is about acquiring the information that a teacher or a textbook has deemed important; there is little time for wrestling with problems or wondering about possibilities. Students rarely get knocked over by a new idea or snuffed by an opposing view. In addition to the disconnect between learners and things learned, there stands a barrier between students and the learning process. Teachers present all of the material and make all of the decisions. Learning is a thing that is done *to* students, not something that they actively participate in. The "greatly plain" classroom, if you will, is neat, orderly, and safe, yet detached and disconnected.

A "collaborative classroom" model, on the other hand, seeks to remove the barriers between students and their learning, inviting students to take an active role in the classroom. Though the word collaborate derives from two Latin words meaning "together" and "work," a collaborative model does not denote that students learn everything in groups. Nor does the idea of students participating in the learning process signify that the classroom ought to be a democracy. The teacher is still in charge, and her expertise is essential to the learning process.

Whereas writers often use the term "collaborative classroom," I prefer "collaborative atmosphere." To teach collaboratively, teachers do not have to reshape the entire classroom or completely metamorphose their teaching style. Though the appearance of the classroom or the teaching may change as a teacher becomes more comfortable, it is usually best to make those modifications gradually. The term "atmosphere" is intended to remind us that collaboration is pursued not for its own sake but as a way to expand opportunities which deepen the learning and heighten a desire to learn.

We're going to investigate the collaborative model because it holds a viable solution for unmotivated learners, one that supports heart-centered teaching. A collaborative atmosphere regards students as humans; it presumes that they have thoughts and questions of their own and acknowledges that those ideas truly matter. In a book that is not fundamentally about teaching strategies, however, we will have to settle for an overview of collaboration in the classroom.[1] After examining two elements of this approach, we will face some of the challenges. Any teaching style that takes into account the created nature of humans must also recognize sinful nature. For good reason, many fear that involving students in their learning would turn the classroom into a kind of zoo. How does one manage a collaborative classroom, especially with difficult students? How is discipline handled? We will examine issues like these here and in later chapters.

Let's begin, then, with a short survey of collaborative learning. In the context of heart-centered teaching, collaboration is largely a matter of making connections: connecting students with the subject matter and connecting them with the learning process. Let's look at each of these components in turn.

Students and Subject

One "gateway to learning" is the teacher's way of communicating with students, and a serious obstruction to this gateway could be called a

---

1 For a detailed description of the collaborative classroom and its benefits for teaching Christianly, I suggest John Van Dyk's *Craft* book. Van Dyk, J. (2005). *The craft of Christian teaching*. Sioux Center, Iowa: Dordt Press.

"teacher tone." This tone is the mode our voices default to when we have a lesson to "get through" or a chapter to "cover." It is difficult to describe the sound of a teacher tone in writing, but the impression it gives its hearers is that learning is a chore rather than something that could change the way you see the world, or even the way you live your life. A teacher tone conveys that the speaker does not personally believe in the importance of what is taught. The lesson is presented only because it is there, not because the material means something. To draw students in, it helps to be enthusiastic, of course. Yet not everyone has the energy to display enthusiasm all of the time. The gateway to a collaborative atmosphere is broader than a teacher's get-up-and-go. Though a person may seek the attention of students with an animated approach, heart-centered teaching acknowledges that the teachable moment often comes about through soft speaking and moments of quiet reflection.

While most teachers ask questions to involve students in learning, collaboration begins to happen when some of the questions become more open-ended. An open-ended or divergent question gets the students thinking about something instead of merely fishing for the right answer. "Can you think of another way to solve a problem like that?" "Why do you suppose the main character in this novel doesn't like her sister's boyfriend?" "What sort of experiment would prove what you just said?" "What kinds of elements made this report fun to read?" "I wonder why the people of that country choose to live this way?"

If students do not want to involve themselves with open-ended questions, a teacher should look for reasons instead of dismissing the strategy or writing off the class. Does the teacher sincerely listen to the responses of the students? When an answer seems off-base, does a teacher gently nudge the student to examine his thinking, or does she quickly call on the next person? Are people allowed to make mistakes here? Does the teacher welcome new ways of thinking about things? Do the questions themselves really matter to students of this age group or setting?

In an atmosphere that welcomes risk-taking and divergent thinking, students often begin to ask questions of their own. Whereas this student initiation may feel immensely rewarding to a teacher, one seeking to enhance collaboration would take care not to supply an answer every time. She might pass the question along to the larger group or possibly even ask the person who ventures an answer to support his thinking in some way. Students connect more with their learning when they begin to talk with each other about the subject at hand, instead of communicating only with the teacher.

Moreover, whereas a challenge to someone's point of view would seem threatening in a traditional classroom, within a collaborative climate students are encouraged to respectfully question the ideas and assumptions of others, even those held by the teacher. One of the reasons students appear to stop thinking as they progress through school is that they are not allowed to question, to argue, or to defend. They learn from teachers who assert opinions as if they were facts and who become defensive when their ideas are challenged. In addition, the inability of students to work through their differences stems in part from learning that arguments are more about winning than about searching for the truth.

An atmosphere that welcomes "rational disagreements" enhances authentic community, which we examined in the last chapter. It brings to light the truth that, as individual persons, we often see things differently. Whereas some may dismiss this view as postmodernist whimsy, what we are talking about here is not the arrogant slant of postmodernism, which suggests that truth is whatever you want it to be. Rather it's the unassuming side, reminding us that we see through a glass dimly. Because none of us sees a complete picture of reality by ourselves, we need each other to test and sometimes reshape our views. A collaborative atmosphere grows respect among students whenever it demonstrates that our value as persons does not diminish if we concede that someone else may be correct or have a better idea.

At a deeper level, teachers teach collaboratively when they allow the questions and ideas of students to shape learning experiences. Inquiry learning, a teaching strategy where the teacher uses the questions and hypotheses of students as launching points for investigation, is commonly limited only to the study of science. However, it can also be implemented as a way to connect students with their learning in other areas. For example, a teacher might introduce the learning experience with an attention-getter, such as photos, objects, or a story. Later, after inviting the class to raise questions about the topic, the teacher works those questions into the outline and activities of the unit, or even uses the questions to shape the entire direction of the study. [2] Shared praxis, a teaching method developed by Paulo Freire and Thomas Groome, begins a learning experience by asking students to share their ideas or their views regarding the topic. Later, after the teacher has presented information about the topic,

---

2   When assigning reading, teachers can ask students to generate their own ideas and questions for the follow-up discussion. Ironically perhaps, the most difficult students to motivate in teacher-led discourses often raise some of the most insightful comments and questions in discussions where both students and teacher are responsible for contributing.

the students are invited to share how their views and possibly their actions would change as a result of the learning.

While teaching strategies like these remove barriers between students and their learning, one key to maintaining a collaborative atmosphere is variety. Even direct instruction, which might seem out of place given the discussion we have just had, plays a vital role within a collaborative setting. The chief question to ask is not "How can I use collaboration for this learning experience?" but instead "How can I plan my teaching in a way that will connect the students with their learning?"

Students and Process

A collaborative atmosphere takes into account not only students' questions and ideas about the things they are learning but also their thoughts about how they learn best. Motivational theorists have long demonstrated the reality of control as a basic human need. When we have no say over what is expected of us, we become resentful, or we look for ways to take control. Unfortunately, the choices people make to recapture control in their lives are often negative or destructive, ranging from passive resistance to turning others against those in authority.

Allowing for input on decisions about the classroom can be a scary notion, especially in a room dominated by difficult students. Yet, a certain amount of "shared authority" is a vital part of heart-centered learning, not just for the self-motivated but also for the kinds of kids who make us earn our pay. In all honesty, allowing for input from students is particularly crucial in redirecting a self-willed group, as ironic as this may seem. So let's work through some of the difficulties of connecting students with process.

First, there are legitimate reasons to feel defensive about student input. As a beginning teacher, you're justly concerned about establishing some authority in the classroom, and students who question you seem to threaten that authority. On the other hand, if you are an established professional who takes your work seriously, you've already devoted thought to your teaching strategies and classroom procedures. What gives children the right to suggest a better way? Perhaps your students have implied that the teacher down the hall is more fun, and you feel as if you can't "compete" with that person's teaching style. Or, maybe the obstacle is not defensiveness at all; you just don't have time to put up with a bunch of whiny, bellyaching students.

On the flip-side of the collaboration coin, students can have a limited view of what school ought to be like, especially if they lack experience with collaboration. This is why students' initial ideas about process often fall under the categories of wanting to do less work and have more fun.

Defensiveness in a teacher and misguided perceptions among students are serious obstacles, yet there are ways to work through them if we're committed to heart-centered teaching. One solution is to provide a format where suggestions and concerns may be voiced in respectful ways. Some make a suggestion box available or welcome students to approach them with classroom-related issues in private. Others invite students to take out a paper and write their ideas about learning at the beginning of a unit, or set aside an amount of time for an open discussion on how the class should approach a learning topic.

Teachers who ask children to journal regularly create a space where student feedback merely becomes part of the culture. Still others invite students to evaluate their effectiveness as teachers at the same time that teachers are performing assessment work for the students. (Responding to students who vent their complaints will be addressed in Chapter Twelve).

There are also ways to help students who think that school should involve less work and more fun. Taking students' ideas seriously does not mean that you cater to every whim. Rather, collaboration should be treated as a double opportunity: first, to demonstrate your own commitment to quality teaching and second, to broaden your students' view of what learning looks like. Over time, students can be trained to recognize the sorts of suggestions that are worth raising. Can they convince you, for instance, that their idea would enhance the learning? Does the suggestion preserve or strengthen an atmosphere where students feel safe and where all have an opportunity to learn? If a suggestion sports a whiny tone and threatens to spoil the atmosphere, a bit of light-hearted humor may appropriately offset the remark. For teachers dedicated to maintaining a positive atmosphere, a rule against public complaining is not a bad idea.

It's painful and frustrating when students don't want to learn, or when they would rather be in someone else's classroom than yours. Careful steps toward a collaborative climate have often helped me through the murk of uncooperative classes. Though I could recount half a dozen examples, one case in particular stands out in my mind. The students of that class weren't belligerent; they were just unresponsive. Neither my enthusiasm nor the variety that I added to my teaching strategies were enough to ignite their interest. My most successful lesson openers for other classes were met with sighs and groans among the students in this group.

Finally I told the class that my energy tank was running on reserve.

I was doing my best to teach well, but they had to try, too. I invited the students to quietly write down their own frustrations or their ideas and hand them to me. Reluctant to know their true thoughts, I put off reading the papers until later that evening. The most common suggestions— "play review games" and "have more fun in class"—were disheartening at first. So the kids wanted to be entertained. Wasn't I already bending over backward to make learning enjoyable?

I planned a tactful yet firm response. School ought to be meaningful and enjoyable, yes, but it's not primarily about having fun. Moreover, in my years of teaching I had never really experienced an effective review game. At best, contests only seemed to separate those who have mastered the information from those who have not.

Next morning, though, I wasn't quite so sure. I still felt that I was right, but rejecting ideas that I had solicited would further unravel the students' trust in me. Perhaps we could compromise. So that day I told them that, at their suggestion, we would try a review game before our next test. However, if the group did not average 85 percent or higher on the test, we would not be able to play a review game the next time around. True to my word, I used a game for review a week later and the class averaged 90 percent, a substantial increase over previous assessments. It was indeed a moment that we could all celebrate.

Additional suggestions were also incorporated eventually, though not arbitrarily. I made it clear that each idea had to prove its sustainability. Any proposal that did not prove to advance the learning could not be continued. I can't say that my problems with the class evaporated in a week, or even in a month. However, over the course of time, I did notice a significant improvement in the general attitude. At first the students seemed motivated to learn only when I was acting on a suggestion they had proposed. After awhile, though, they began to respond more positively to my teaching style; they didn't seem to need as much "control" over their learning as they had initially desired. In a collaborative atmosphere, it is not just the teaching methods themselves that connect students with their learning. Motivation also comes from allowing students a voice in the teaching and learning process.

Obstructions or Opportunities?
Now back to a couple of questions I raised earlier. Involving students in their learning is fine, but how does a teacher accomplish everything that needs to be done? And how does one approach classroom management in a collaborative atmosphere?

With increasing requirements imposed on teachers, it's natural to feel anxious about covering all of the material. Yet responding to that fear by hustling students from one topic to the next without time for curiosity or wonder erects barriers that keep students disengaged from learning.

Teachers wanting to connect students with their learning soon realize that they cannot get through as many topics as they could otherwise. Rather than see this problem as a roadblock, committed teachers recognize an opportunity to strengthen the curriculum. Seeing themselves as professionals, they treat the textbook as a resource rather than as a "manual," making deliberate choices about what would best serve their students. Certain topics merit study of greater depth, for example, while other topics can be trimmed or pruned out because of undue repetition or lack of relevance. Teachers working toward a collaborative atmosphere make space for connecting in their programs of study by teaching fewer topics with greater depth.

Teaching collaboratively also affects one's approach to classroom management. A teacher committing to a collaborative atmosphere from the beginning of a school year would likely invite the students to assist in setting some of the rules for the classroom. Naturally the teacher would use that time to set the tone for the year: whereas student input is welcome, the focus will be on those behaviors that preserve an atmosphere of learning. Further, the teacher might have rules of her own that are not negotiable.

Rule enforcement in a collaborative atmosphere is not always a straightforward matter. When students begin to connect with their learning, for example, it is not uncommon for them to forget their inhibitions and involve themselves in what is going on. A casual observer visiting a collaborative classroom might at first wonder at the amount of talking that students do. Occasionally a student may even speak out of turn, without reprimand. If the visitor were paying any attention at all, though, he or she would soon realize that the talking was not a free-for-all but a dialogue, a conversation among students and a teacher exploring a topic, debating an issue, or solving a problem. How does one maintain a consistent discipline policy in this type of setting?

In an atmosphere that values learning and respect, consistency revolves around a bigger picture than just the rules. The rules that the teacher (and students) set promote the desired atmosphere. However, in a situation where it would impede the atmosphere, a rule may be set aside. Take, for example, the moment when a teacher and the students are so caught up in a discussion that a couple of people forget to raise their hands before speaking. It's okay for the teacher to make a judgment call in situations like these. Reminding or reprimanding students concerning a particular rule in the middle of a conversation may break the momentum of the learning. If too many students begin to talk out of turn, or if some voices aren't being heard, then obviously the teacher needs to enforce the rule. "Consistency" in a collaborative atmosphere centers around an atmosphere of respect and learning, rather than around the rule system itself.

Perhaps you remember the story about my first class, the one with the students who disrupted almost uncontrollably? The occasional serious comment or question was so welcome that I couldn't bear to respond to those in the same way that I reacted to the other interferences. Yet choosing not to reprimand those who made positive contributions without raising their hands seemed a terrible unfairness to the students who had been penalized for visiting or for arguing. Knowing what I do today (and possessing the confidence that I have today), such a class does not seem nearly as intimidating. When we talk about our classroom rules, I generally ask the students why talking out of turn gets in the way of learning and makes the classroom an unpleasant place to be. I also ask if there are times when it might be okay to make a comment or ask a question out of turn. Understanding depends on maturity level, of course, but most students are able to figure out that consistency can be more about the learning than about the rule itself.

Conclusion

A heart-centered classroom climate has a collaborative atmosphere. It acknowledges the created nature of learners as humans, taking into account their ideas and their questions. It also takes seriously the fallen side of human nature and works for redemption by guiding students into an understanding of what learning looks like and teaching them how to work alongside other learners.

All of the ideas we've discussed so far—tightening the connections between teachers and students, cultivating a supportive learning community, and breaking down the walls that separate students from subject—these undertakings create the optimal conditions for diminishing a contrary nature in students while growing the inclinations we hope for in students.

Despite a favorable climate, agreeable attitudes are still susceptible to the encroaching weeds of willfulness and negativity. We are going to take a look now at addressing discipline problems in a heart-centered climate. As with the chapters leading up to this point, the goal in heart-centered discipline is not merely getting kids to behave the way we want them to: our aim is to propagate love, cooperation, and a desire to learn.

PART THREE:
HEART-CENTERED DISCIPLINE

CHAPTER 7:
GUIDING WITH GRACE

Getting Them Back

When I started teaching, our school owned two reel-to-reel film projectors that we could check out and take to our classrooms for showing movies. "The Gray Machine" was brand-new and state of the art; it loaded film tape automatically and even shut off by itself when the movie was over. The other projector, dubbed "Old Green," was not self-feeding, and sometimes the tape would come off the gears on the machine. Then its picture would shake, and the scholarly voice of the narrator would suddenly morph into something like Winnie the Pooh talking with mouthwash in the back of his throat.

In an indirect way, though, Old Green was more dependable than The Gray Machine. Our handy administrator could usually tinker Old Green back into commission when things went haywire. The Gray Machine, on the other hand, often had to be sent in for repairs. People who signed up for Gray ahead of time took a gamble that it might be out of service on the day they needed it.

Of course anyone who signed up for Old Green still faced the problem of transporting it from the media center to the classroom. Each piece of media equipment had a cart that went with it, and Old Green's cart was notorious. Its loud, squeaky wheels constantly veered to the right. You could compensate by applying pressure to the left, but just when you least expected it, the wheels would concede and swing the cart into oncoming traffic.

Coming down the hall, the outfit sounded like a wild turkey in mating season. People who worked at the school recognized the noise and got out of the way, but visitors were sometimes caught off-guard. I never actually crashed into anybody, but it did look as if I had tried a couple of times. How do you explain yourself to a complete stranger when you almost shoved a cart into her stomach?

It goes without saying that neither a kick nor a well-deserved scolding would have solved the problem. A firm but patient hand was the only way to keep Old Green on course. Eventually I learned to work with the cart's personality, pushing it half-sideways. This trick allowed the wheels to veer as they wanted while the cart moved ahead. Though the maneuver looked kind of odd, coaxing the cart along that way became easier than fighting it.

That image of Old Green's cart portrays the difference between two different approaches to discipline, *reacting* and *redirecting*. When students behave as they ought to, they are moving forward, headed in the right direction. When they break the rules or refuse to cooperate, they are veering off course. You might say that both the teacher who reacts and the teacher who redirects want to "get students back," though each would interpret that phrase differently. The reactive person sees discipline as an exercise in evening the scores; one wrong turn deserves another. A redirecting teacher, on the other hand, uses discipline to guide students back, back to the right path. The image below may help to make this idea more clear.

The difference between reacting and redirecting lies not necessarily in the choice of one particular method over another. Rather, the distinction is found in the principles that guide the discipline and in the atmosphere where that discipline is carried out. The list below compares various elements of the two styles.

Reacting	Redirecting
Focuses on the **past**	Focuses on the **future**
Makes the student **pay**	Encourages the student to **think**
Considers what students **deserve**	Takes into account what students **need**
Draws the teacher into **contention**	Allows a teacher to **guide**

Often driven by **emotions**	Driven by the **mind**
Limited to **threats** and **punishments**	Employs a **repertoire** of strategies
Scrutinizes only the **behavior**	Considers what may lie **beneath the surface**

We will look at each of these elements more closely as we make our way through this section of the book. To summarize, though, reactive discipline seeks mostly to exterminate misbehavior (as indicated by the stop sign), while redirecting encourages right behavior (as shown by the sign with the arrow). Redirecting teachers do not content themselves with merely getting the wrong behavior to desist. Instead they want to help wrong-doers see things differently and to behave differently as a result. Ultimately, they seek a change of heart as they nudge students closer to the path of what is right or good.

A Rebuttal from Mr. React

A letter showed up in the mail about a week after an article of mine had been published in a magazine for Christian teachers. My article used two hypothetical teachers to demonstrate some of the differences between reacting and redirecting. I had argued that a gentle approach to discipline is often more effective than a harsh response.[1]

The writer of the letter was infuriated—I could almost smell the smoke from his pen when I tore open the envelope. In the letter he asserted that the sinful nature drives misbehavior and that misbehaving students need threats and punishments, not "counseling" (the term he applied to my description of discipline). He called me a secular humanist and asked why people like me could not accept plain-spoken biblical truth. Some of the Proverbs, he reminded, speak even of corporal punishment.

The letter was unsettling, but it was also helpful in "prodding" me to reexamine my views and measure them against the standards of Scripture. After some study and reflection, I wrote a letter of response to thank the person for his remarks and to offer some counterarguments to his views.

Yes, I was familiar with some of the Proverbs that speak of corporal punishment, such as "He who spares the rod hates his son, but he who loves him is careful to discipline him" (13:24). However, I couldn't ignore other verses in Proverbs which speak of a softer approach: "A gentle answer turns away wrath, but a harsh word stirs up anger" (15:1). And King David, in Psalm 23, actually finds comfort in the rod of his Shepherd,

---

1   Bandstra, A. "Control without coercion." (2002-2003). *Christian School Education*, *VI*, 23-24. In that article, "punishment and discipline" were the actual terms I used instead of "reacting and redirecting."

One who guides (not beats) him in paths of righteousness. Galatians 6 teaches, "[I]f someone is caught in a sin, you who are spiritual should restore him gently," and II Timothy 2, echoing that advice: disciplining "in the hope that God will grant them repentance leading to a knowledge of the truth."

Finally, in the gospels Jesus rarely uses a harsh approach when he confronts people about wrong. Consider his treatment of the woman who was to be stoned for adultery, his consideration for a swindler named Zaccheus, and his reinstatement of the disciple Peter after Peter's hurtful denial. Though Jesus (justly) flew into a rage when he cleared the temple, and though he had some choice words for the Pharisees, his overall message carried a tone of grace and forgiveness.

The Bible leaves room for strong discipline, to be sure, but I have difficulty with any kind of response that is vindictive, which looks for revenge. Our debt for sin has already been settled through Christ's atoning work on the cross. Of course, if misbehavior causes damage, that damage ought to be recompensed in some way, but the sin itself does not need to be paid for all over again. Salvation is a gift of grace; it's free. Further, if we take Jesus' teachings and his parables about forgiveness seriously, we are called to pass on the grace we have freely received to those around us. Grace is not something we *give*; it is something we *share*.

Yet we also know that this gift is not a license to go on sinning so that grace may increase.[2] A gift that enables someone to do wrong is no gift at all. Even though grace sets the repentant free from their guilt, it should also help to free people from their wrongful ways.

Guiding With Grace

Sharing grace in discipline begs two questions. Do heart-centered teachers withhold grace when it's time to get firm? If wrong does not have to be paid for, how do we hold students accountable for their actions? First, caring teachers don't turn off the grace spigot when they torque up the pressure. Compassionate teachers really never stop showing grace because it's always about what others need, not what they deserve. Let me explain it this way.

Sometimes students need to feel discomfort in order to be convinced that changes are necessary in their lives. In a heart-centered classroom, however, neither the consequence nor the teacher's displeasure is a punitive measure. The goal is to get the student back on track, not to drive him or her away. In this sense, even firm discipline is an act of grace

2   Romans 6:1.

if it aims to keep students from a harmful path. Children who slough off in their work will miss out on important skills and information. Young people who mouth off to their teachers are likely to have run-ins with authority at work or with the law. Those who acquire what they want by bullying are headed for a lonely life. In some cases, it would be easier for teachers to ignore these kinds of problems or to give up on students with bad habits. When teachers care enough to show disappointment or to impose stiff consequences with the hope of turning students from a destructive road, teachers impart grace.

In response to the second question, let's think about the way grace comes into play when students need to be held accountable for their behavior. If others lay into us for a misdeed we have committed, we naturally protect ourselves by making excuses or shifting the blame. It is not necessarily the right choice, but it is the instinctive choice. There's a greater chance that I will take responsibility for my actions if I can be permitted to see my wrong for what it is without being shamed.

As I said a moment ago, grace not only relieves people from guilt; it also aims to free them from a wrongful path. If students are to experience heart-felt repentance, they have to get their head around the trouble resulting from their misbehavior. They need to own up to their mistakes and make the necessary amends. Or they may need to recognize that their sin is a tyrant and begin to desire the true freedom of life in Christ. Harshness encourages students to erect barriers, to justify their choices, and to resist genuine change. By contrast, gentleness invites those disciplined to take responsibility—to be accountable—for their behavior.

How do imposed consequences factor into guiding with grace? Imposed consequences serve as deterrents for misbehavior, yet teachers who levy consequences in a context of grace aim for a couple of ideals. When possible, they choose a consequence that matches the wrongdoing and opens the door to change or to rectify the problem. A student who is chronically tardy, for instance, might be required to organize himself by cleaning out his desk or locker. The one who threw paper wads in class would be asked to sweep out the room, and so on. Finally, teachers who give consequences with grace also treat their students as persons, without attacking or belittling. Even when the misbehavior calls for a severe consequence, that measure can still be imposed in a tone that preserves one's dignity.

Regardless of whether the most appropriate response is to be firm or gentle, grace also calls for forgiveness. On the one hand, forgiveness implies "forgetting" certain things about the past. When we forgive, we set people free from guilt by treating them with kindness. However, forgiveness does not prevent us from adapting our teaching or management practices. Teachers of wayward students regularly make changes to curb misbehavior, for example: they move students around in the seating arrangement, adjust classroom procedures, or limit freedoms that have been abused. They may even alter their teaching style so that they can watch certain students more closely. But the one constant in a heart-centered classroom is the teacher's love for the kids. Teachers demonstrate forgiveness when they continue to treat their students with respect despite the consequences that student misbehavior brings about.

But That Isn't Fair!

In the discussion of grace and consequences, another question often arises: how do classroom management systems work in a heart-centered classroom? For teachers who see corrective discipline as retribution rather than as an act of guiding, one-size-fits-all formulas for rules and consequences are attractive. Classroom management is about keeping the accounts paid; no one makes an issue about fairness because everyone is treated the same. In heart-centered classrooms, though, management is not always a black-and-white undertaking.

The logic behind flexibility in a heart-centered teacher's approach to management comes from an additional concept about grace. So far we have seen that grace involves offering what students need instead of what they deserve, respectfully encouraging wrongdoers to take responsibility for their actions, and imposing consequences in a context of forgiveness. Another reality about grace is that it meets students where they are. We know that all students cannot achieve the same standard of behavior. Each young person has a unique set of shortcomings and challenges to overcome, and each is at a different place in understanding and maturity. Furthermore, a certain consequence that leads to positive change in some students could actually grow resistance or discouragement in others. Lastly, discipline situations can also vary. One student is late for class because she talked too long in the cafeteria. Another misses the bell because she stopped to help someone who dropped her books in the hallway.

Because students and situations vary, heart-centered teachers use care in designing rules and consequences for the classroom. Some address differences among students by simplifying the rules and keeping their number to a minimum. "Do only what is helpful," for example.[3] Others, who feel that they need to spell things out a little more clearly,

---

3 Van Dyk, J. (2005). *The craft of Christian teaching*. Sioux Center, Iowa: Dordt Press.

publish a list of possible consequences for each rule. When a rule is broken, the teacher can take various factors into account before choosing the best response.[4]

Teachers who choose not to operate according to a one-size-fits-all system live with a certain amount of tension. Each discipline situation presents several factors to consider: the maturity level of the student, possible reasons for the misbehavior, and what response would be most effective, to name a few. On top of the decision-making, heart-centered teachers may also have to deal with those who believe that they have been treated unfairly. That strain is a lot less likely, however, when the conditions of a heart-centered classroom are in place. Teachers who have worked to build the trust of their students, for example, have less difficulty convincing those students that fairness and equality are not always the same.

The pressure of needing to be fair is also less of a factor when teachers consistently think of discipline as something children need instead of something they deserve. Let me share an example. One teacher says to a couple of chatty students, "I'm going to have to separate you because you are getting in the way of each other's learning. We talked about this problem yesterday, and it's still not working out." This teacher believes, and conveys, that a different arrangement would be more conducive to their learning needs. Another teacher says, "You have had enough warnings about talking out of turn in class. Now pick up your things and move." This teacher sees the measure as a punishment that the talkative students deserve and communicates it as such.

Let's take it a step further now. A few minutes later, two other students begin to talk quietly with each other in the same class. As it turns out, one of them was re-explaining a concept to a neighbor. The second teacher, who framed his discipline of the earlier talkative students as a penalty, now will have to decide if these two students also deserve a penalty, and his choice might invite criticism.

All things considered, the teacher who consistently imparts grace by providing what students need is less susceptible to fault-finding than the teacher who attempts to uniformly extract the payments that students owe.

Grace and Sacrifice

A final thought to examine is the link between grace and sacrifice. In Chapter Three we saw that Paul calls believers to offer themselves as living sacrifices. It was there that we first connected with the idea that

---

4 Curwin, R. L. & and Mendler, A. N. (1988). *Discipline with dignity*. Association for Supervision and Curriculum Development.

teachers respond to this call when they absorb the negativity in wayward students—their unfriendliness, apathy, or antagonism—as they seek to meet needs rather than settle scores.

There are additional kinds of sacrifices that teachers make, though, when they exemplify Christ in their approach to discipline. Professor Donovan Graham highlights a number of them in his book *Teaching Redemptively*. Teachers who endeavor to understand misbehaving students, for example, "may need to sacrifice efficiency, control, and comfort for [themselves]."[5] A colleague of mine recently demonstrated these kinds of sacrifices during a confrontation with a disruptive student. After the teacher stated the purpose of their meeting, the child suddenly broke down in tears and began to talk about his dad's recent injury and the family's financial burden that had resulted from the injury. The teacher listened as the young man shared the stress that dominated his home life. Then she expressed her concern and offered to pray for the child and his family. Despite the burden that this child carried, though, his classroom behavior was still inexcusable, and she told him so gently but firmly.

How did that particular confrontation reveal sacrifice? In pausing to listen before responding, the teacher gave up time that she had hoped to devote to her other work. She also sacrificed a certain amount of control by allowing the story to adjust the direction of the confrontation. Finally, in choosing to understand the child's pain, she gave up comfort for herself. Guessing from what I know about this teacher's personality, I picture her eyes welling up with tears as the young man's story unfolded.

Following Christ in the process of redirecting may involve other kinds of sacrifices as well. Graham goes on to list several of them:

> Entering into the life of troublesome children also causes us to sacrifice our sense of position and well being. At times, correcting them may cause us to sacrifice our sense of being loved by them. Any effort to deal with problem children as true human beings instead of as objects to be controlled will cost us time and energy and will likely put us into a situation where we cannot be sure of the outcome (loss of human control of the situation). It may even cost us our reputations (or our jobs) if dealing with the children in these ways does not reap the results others demand.[6] (249)

Even though grace is given away for free, it often requires a payment from those who share it. As theologian and martyr Dietrich Bonhoeffer

---

5   Graham, D. (2009). *Teaching redemptively: Bringing grace and truth into your classroom.* Colorado Springs, Colorado: Purposeful Design Publications. P. 249.

6   Graham, D. Ibid.

once observed, grace is costly.[7]

The idea of sacrifice in redirecting wayward students may seem unpleasant, especially if we value efficiency and control in our classrooms. Yet after seeing the benefits that grace provides, the pattern of offering oneself for the restoration of others becomes an easier road to travel. The confrontation I described a moment ago, for example, marked a turning point in the child's behavior. To be sure, there were occasional setbacks, but the overall change in his attitude was positive.

Because no approach or technique carries a guarantee when applied to student attitudes, however, the higher reward in sacrificing oneself in discipline is not found in seeing the returns from your labor. Rather, it is in the joy of presenting a living picture of Christ to your students.

Conclusion

We have now compared two different approaches to discipline: reacting and redirecting. Heart-centered teachers make every effort to redirect students, to point them in a new direction. They tend to focus on where students are headed rather than where they have been, and they think about what young people need instead of what their deeds merit.

Teachers who redirect believe that a gentle response is usually more effective than a severe response. This presumption, we saw, leads to questions about accountability. Some suspect that students who don't get what they deserve will remain stuck in their sinful ways.

Teachers who follow Christ take a different view of accountability. The grace we have first received in Christ is a gift we are called to pass on to the people around us. Grace releases people from their guilt, but it also invites them to take ownership of their wrong so that they can make the necessary repairs, or so that they can leave the wrong behind and take a new path. A person who has been shown grace is usually in a better position to take responsibility—or to be accountable—for wrong than a person who is required to pay. In addition, heart-centered correction meets students where they are. It doesn't expect all students to achieve the same standard of behavior. Yet it also graciously does not leave them where they are; heart-centered discipline expects growth.

Finally, grace often requires sacrifice, especially when grace is bestowed in ways that lead others back to the right path. Even though the idea of sacrifice may be unpleasant, the cost seems less burdensome when people find their greatest joy in modeling their lives after the pattern of their Lord.

---

7 Bonhoffer, D. (1995). *The cost of discipleship.* New York: Touchstone.

CHAPTER 8:
STUBBORN PATIENCE

Love is Patient

Having spent a class period observing in my room, a college student stopped to thank me on her way out the door. "You are a patient person," she added as she turned to go. I never know quite how to read that sort of comment. Was the person impressed by my composure? Or did she actually find my room somewhat chaotic and wonder how I could appear so oblivious to it all?

I have not always been known as a patient person. The wall that separated my first classroom from the teachers' lounge was a temporary one that stopped sound about as well as chicken wire holds back the wind. I did not know just how thin the wall was, though, until another person on our faculty eventually told me that many of the threats I yelled at my students each day were clearly heard by the teachers who drank coffee next door during their recess breaks. Embarrassing. My management style today, thankfully, is a testimony that patience is not strictly an inherited quality, like eye color or freckles. Patience in teaching is more of a conviction than a personality trait, and needs to be practiced if it is to flourish.

The title of this section borrows from the Apostle Paul's words about love in I Corinthians 13. Many teachers rightly claim that they love their students. If we were pressed to explain what it means to love someone, most of us would probably agree that love desires to do what is best for another person. Patience is demonstrated when teachers choose to override their emotions, at least for a time, to enable themselves to make wise decisions and to carry out those decisions in loving ways.

A Culture of Hurry

Unfortunately, North American culture conditions most of us to be anything but patient. Why save up to buy a new sofa next year, for example, if I can take it home on credit today? Rather than muddling through the chapters of a long book, I could just watch the movie. Many kinds of products encourage a lack of patience too, telling us that the personal improvements we desire can be attained rapidly and through minimal effort. The irony of some of their claims, especially those related to physical shrinkage or spiritual growth, is almost amusing. "Effortlessly Thin" said one magazine cover in our grocery store. Just above the caption, a smiling woman holds a salad that looks like something our neighbors' pet rabbit would probably turn down. Christian devotionals are often written for impatient people, too. One book cover I saw proclaimed: "designed to encourage and foster spiritual maturity." Its title was *The One-Minute Bible 4 Students.*

If we like to see immediate results, if we are not used to waiting for things, then an occupation like teaching can be a frustrating task. Even though many of the physical objects in our lives are changeable or *ex*changeable, people are not quickly transformed. By threatening or rewarding, we may change certain behaviors, but we cannot so easily control how students think or feel. In most cases we cannot effortlessly cause students to respect us, or to get along with others, or to care about learning. We may be able, through time, to influence the inner notions of the students we are responsible for, but these kinds of transformations do not typically happen in a day, or even in a month. And that inability to bring about swift change can be frustrating.

Patient Versus Permissive

Before we move on, I need to address a common misunderstanding about patience. Patience is sometimes confused with permissiveness. Folks assume that, in order to be patient, one must somehow learn to tolerate, to "put up with," wrongdoing. It is almost as if those who show patience with misbehaving students voluntarily relinquish some of their authority. Actually, the kind of patient teacher I am attempting to describe is no more tolerant of misdeeds than the impatient teacher. The difference is in what the patient teacher believes, namely that he or she is a teacher and not a contender. Teachers who retain control of themselves are much more likely to gain control in a discipline situation, able to encourage their students along a different path.

I offer some examples to demonstrate the differences between a response that lacks patience and a response that exhibits patience. These examples are not intended to prescribe discipline strategies, but instead to illustrate that patience is not the same as permissiveness.

Second-grade teacher Kathy sees two third-graders running through the hall on their way out to recess. It's the second time this week for one of them. Kathy ushers them to the sign about proper hallway behavior and asks them to read the rules aloud. Hands on the hips, she gives an extra scolding to the one she had caught earlier and then tells them that their punishment will be to walk the same stretch of hallway two times before they go outside. When Karl huffs and starts to complain, she cuts him off and threatens a further consequence. After their second trip past her, she glares at them and shakes her head before returning to her room.

In the corresponding "patient" example, Alyssa is the teacher in the hallway where the students are running. Careful to avoid a sarcastic tone, she asks them why running in the hallway is against the rules and listens to their response. Alyssa tells the students that they will need to "practice" the rule by walking through the hallway twice before they may go. When Karl tries to argue about the absurdity of this consequence, she smiles and assures him that he will be fine. Inside Alyssa is pleased about the objection; it's a sign that he will probably think twice before running through her hallway again. As the students make their two practice trips back down the hallway, Alyssa enjoys a few sips of coffee from the cup in her hand. She offers a sincere thank you after they've completed their second pass, then asks if they are going to remember to walk from now on. Satisfied with their response, Alyssa returns to her room.

In my second example, the sophomores in Ted's biology class are working in pairs dissecting a frog. As he meanders around the room, answering questions and offering advice, he begins to notice that Samantha and Erin aren't taking the activity seriously. Every minute or two, they erupt in loud laughter, disrupting everyone's concentration. The guys in the vicinity, enjoying the drama, make comments and add to the laughter. Samantha is now holding, at arm's length, an impaled organ on the end of a probe. Pinching her nose with her other hand, she howls with disgust. Erin covers her own mouth and nose and laughs along at the scene her teammate is making. Because Jasmine likes dissecting, she steps over from another table to make the next incision for them, but neither of the girls bothers even to watch the work she is doing.

After a few stern looks, Ted has had enough. He walks over to the girls and slams his instruction manual down, causing several students to jump. "You girls are acting like third-graders. So far you've done nothing this period except giggle and distract others." Except for the scolding, the room is now silent. Students smirk at each other as Ted goes on about using class time responsibly and respecting the parts of creation. "This whole section is more than half a period behind now. If you two don't start taking this thing seriously and show you can handle working together in class, I'm giving you an assignment to do in your book instead. Then you can come back after school to finish the dissection. Have I made myself clear?"

Once again we insert another teacher into the scenario, Nicholas this time. After making eye contact with the girls and shaking his head "no" a couple of times, Nicholas also has had enough. He walks to their corner and asks them to step out into the hall with him. When a couple of the guys ask where they are going, Nicholas himself replies to the question, explaining that they're taking a short break. He refocuses the students in the classroom on their work, reminding them to be especially careful in the next step.

The transition gives Nicholas just enough time to cool his nerves and to assess what has been happening. Out in the hall, he keeps his eye on the class with frequent looks through his open door. "I'm guessing you two aren't so excited about dissecting?" Laughing sheepishly, the girls agree that they are not. "Well, you probably don't realize this, but we're now about half a period behind the other class because of all the laughing and staring that's been going on in the room." The teacher lets that comment sink in as he looks back into the classroom for several seconds. Turning back to them, he continues, "You don't have to enjoy this, but you do have to do the work. Taking the time to look closely at animals is one way we honor their Maker. Does that make sense to you?" One of the girls nods and the other looks down. "If you're too squeamish to do this project on your own, I'd be glad to help you after school. But to make sure you're continuing to learn something during class, I would have to give you a book assignment to work on for the rest of the period." He lets the girls think about his words as he takes another look back into the classroom.

Turning back to them, he finishes. "You may decide. Do you want to give it another try, or shall I help you later on today?" The girls look at each other for a moment and reply that they will try to continue the activity now. "Sorry," says Samantha quietly as they walk back through the door.

In both scenarios, the consequences remained the same. Even though teachers who show patience often impose different consequences than those who lack patience, I wanted to demonstrate that the biggest difference is not in the consequences themselves but in the teacher's response and in how the consequences are framed. Teachers who use a patient approach choose a way of responding that nudges misbehaving students back to the right path rather than just stopping the behavior that is wrong.

"Initial patience" is the composure that heart-centered teachers often show in their immediate response to misbehavior. Both Alyssa and Nicholas kept their cool with the students who were creating problems. Initial patience is not limitless, though. Patient teachers do not always choose to remain calm and collected. There are times when patient teachers rightly become impatient with students, to get their attention or to reveal the urgency of the need for compliance. As we will see in a few moments, *impatience* and *non-patience* must be distinguished from each other.

It Always Trusts, Always Hopes, Always Perseveres

In regard to the work of getting young people to change their attitudes and behavior, education professor Barb Hoekstra quips, "I'm going to die trying." There's a double meaning in these words, yet both dimensions fit our context here. On the one hand, when we soak up negativity and exchange it with a loving nudge in the right direction, it can seem like we've just inched a step closer to demise. We feel older, more tired, more used up. "Initial patience" is a costly gift to give.[1]

On the other hand, growing new ways of seeing and behaving in students is a slow, deliberate process that really never reaches completion. With the help of God's Spirit, we make inroads, thankfully, but the work goes on until we quit teaching—or die. This reality brings us to the second type of patience.

At the core of heart-centered teachers dwells a longer, steadier attribute that merits our attention. "Stubborn patience" forbears with the deep-seated changes that are needed in others. To start with, it seeks to understand the student before deciding what those changes should be. While stubborn patience may carry in the back of its mind a vision of what the child may become, it loves the child now for what the child is today. Finally, though stubborn patience loves children and young people for who they are, it does not allow them to stay where they are. It perseveres, concurrently working for and expecting growth.

Fusing Patience with Stubbornness

Stubborn patience is a combination of faith and persistence. To illustrate this unity, let me tell you about a mechanic I once knew who had a cer-

---

1   It's ironic, then, that effective teachers seem to retain their vitality for so long. Maybe Christ's statement "whoever loses their life for me and for the gospel will save it" (Mark 8:35) in some way extends to the quality of life on earth as well as our place of eternal destiny.

tain knack with car engines. On a Sunday morning in June of 1991, I was driving through the country to pick up my fiancé for church when my car overheated and stalled. A farmer who had just come out of a wet field with his tractor stopped to offer me a ride. I sat beside him on the fender and fretted about my car—the first I had ever owned—as clods of mud, flung skyward by the tractor tires, made u-turns in the air and rained back down upon us.

The next day the head mechanic at the dealership, where my car had been towed, advised me to junk that old car and buy a newer one. The problem was not repairable, he declared. The man must have noticed the despair on my face when I asked if there was any way of reviving my car. "Well, I guess I could let *Phiz* take a crack at it," he said. Tossing his head toward a thin, grey-bearded man under the hood of a van in the far corner of the shop, he laughed, "That guy is so stubborn, he can fix anything!" Well, Phiz did find a way to patch up my car. Though the engine now made a few noises that it didn't before, I was able to drive my car to the church on my wedding day two weeks later.

Though Phiz was a whiz under the hood, he was human, of course. From what I've been told, his words and wrenches flew against the walls of the shop once in awhile. The quality that set Phiz apart, however, was hope and trust combined with perseverance. Phiz liked cars and motors, but I think he enjoyed the challenging ones most. In his mind, the question was not, "Will this car run again?" but instead, "What will it take to get this car running again?" If Phiz needed stubborn patience with mechanical things which have no personal agendas, how much more do we need stubborn patience with human beings who have the capacity to actively resist us.

At school, teachers with that "Phiz" feature patiently—and stubbornly—refuse to give up on students. They pray fervently that God's Spirit will work through their lessons, through the ways that they interact with the students, and through their methods of discipline; and they operate in the faith that God's Spirit will indeed do so. They do not write students off as unreachable when those students remain untransformed despite much effort and time invested. Instead, they thank God for the smallest changes that occur, in their hearts shouting a silent "Amen" for even the tiniest hint of improvement they see.

Of course culture and home life remain as powerful influences in the lives of our students. In all likelihood, we cannot change the extraneous elements that undermine our efforts at school. Yet within the walls of the school and within the confines of the school day, we have more potential for affecting students' attitudes than we realize. Faith calls us to focus not on the problems but on the possibilities.

Impatience and Non-Patience

We've reached the point now where we can examine the difference between *impatience* and *non-patience*. Patient teachers may sometimes become impatient with troublesome students. Though I'd like to say that the switch is triggered by a rational choice, our humanity often proves otherwise. Sometimes we just lose our patience. In doing so, however, we do not necessarily renounce our heart-centered convictions. Even in impatience, you see, there is expectancy. Patient teachers who occasionally become impatient still look for growth and believe it can occur. This is why those teachers, after showing some impatience, can return to their patient side and continue to encourage difficult students.

Teachers who become *non-patient*, on the other hand, stop anticipating growth. They do not believe that troublesome students can or will change. They decline to recognize that God is still at work in challenging students' lives. You may hear a tone of cynicism or sarcasm in their comments. Teachers lay the blame for classroom problems at the feet of parents, administrators, peer pressure, television, the internet, video games, music, or pop culture at large. They do not patiently keep working for positive change in their students. They do not even *im*patiently work for that change. They have become *non*-patient.

One benefit of age, at least for me, is that stubborn patience has become easier to maintain. For one thing, there is a mellowness that comes through growing older, but it's more than that. Each year that passes, I rack up more and more debt to God's grace. I can see, with some embarrassment, how God and certain people in my life have had to be patient with me. Knowing that they have put up with my sluggish pace of growth makes it easier for me to wait for others. Another reason I stay patient is because I have seen some "hopeless cases" eventually grow into godly men and women—leading businesses, volunteering in the community, and even serving on school boards!

Yes, stubborn patience is more of an attitude than a technique. If we cultivate that attitude, though, it can greatly affect the way we view difficult students and, in turn, affect the way we respond to those students.

Reframing the Behavior Problem as a Learning Problem

When behaviors and the attitudes that drive them are difficult to change, it helps to view the behavior problem as a learning problem. If a student struggles with learning a skill, you typically don't lecture the student on why he should master that skill. If you believe that the new skill is important, and if you are confident that the student has the ability to learn it, you commit yourself to helping that student until he's got it. You might think of a new way to explain it or give the student some extra practice. You might temporarily lower the standard for the child who really struggles, or you might allow additional time, but you wouldn't give up until that person reached the proficiency level of which he is capable. Additionally, you would provide plenty of encouragement along the way.

How does a teaching model change one's approach to discipline? First, you may recall from Chapter Three that the boundary between teaching and discipline is not always distinguishable when a teacher chooses a teaching framework for correction. Even when a heart-centered teacher is not engaged in a disciplinary act, that person continues to teach appropriate behavior. Often this instruction is carried out through modeling rather than through explicit lessons. A teaching approach to discipline includes an ongoing demonstration of the attitudes and behaviors we strive for in students: how we treat each other, how we react to someone who disagrees with us, and how we respond to criticism.

Please also recall that heart-centered discipline does not necessarily remove imposed consequences. Instead it changes the context in which the consequence is given. In the hallway situation with the third-graders, both teachers used the "practice" as a consequence, but Alyssa encouraged and thanked the students. Both biology teachers threatened extra homework, but Nicholas thought of a way to show the effects of the misbehavior before doing so. With just enough words to make his point clear—and no more— he explained the reason for his expectations and the logic behind the consequence. Let's look at a couple other examples of framing behavior problems as learning problems.

First-grade teacher Mr. Gabriel takes time to talk with Kayla who struggles with anger. Sometimes she snaps at kids who tease her and has occasionally resorted to kicking and shoving. Directly after each outburst, Gabriel tells Kayla that they will have to talk, but he allows time for the anger to subside before they meet. Sometimes Mr. Gabriel shares stories of his own struggles with anger and the hurt his flare-ups have caused. The two remind each other of non-aggressive ways people can express disappointment, and they commit themselves to trying harder the next time either of them feels angry. Two days later, when Mr. Gabriel notices the girl avoiding an outburst by choosing one of the reactions they agreed upon, he catches her eye, smiles, and gives the thumbs-up.

He knows that Kayla will probably always struggle with her anger, but he is thankful for the small steps of progress she is making.

Down the hall, three of the trumpeters in Mr. Lim's middle school band aren't taking rehearsals seriously. Despite a couple of confrontations with the teacher, they continue playing when he directs the band to stop, and they disrupt class with their antics and laughter whenever he pauses to work with other sections. Frustrated by their unwillingness to cooperate, the conductor seeks the help of another teacher who has a break at the time this rehearsal meets. The two agree that this teacher will monitor the trio if they need to be removed from the band for part of a rehearsal.

As Mr. Lim fills his trumpeters in on the plan, he points out the problem and shows them that the things they have already tried aren't working. He is confident that they can still learn the songs, but that it may work better if they rehearsed apart from the rest of the group. Mr. Lim explains that the next time it doesn't go well during rehearsal, the students will work on a music-related written assignment, by themselves, in the other teacher's room during the rehearsal. And later in the day, during break time, the students will come back to the band room to work on the songs with Mr. Lim. As he shares this arrangement, the teacher's tone remains calm and sincere, not sarcastic. The intervention is not a "payment plan" for disobedience; it is a plan for making effective learning possible.

When teachers view behavior problems as learning problems, they choose to respond to students on their own terms, not on the students' terms. They teach rather than retaliate and offer encouragement instead of frustration. Is it legitimate practice, though, to apply a teaching model to a discipline problem? Shouldn't we "call a spade a spade" and give students what they've got coming?

Without a doubt, misbehavior is still wrong; it is still *sin*, if you will. To single out misbehaviors as sinful, however, is to ignore the pervasiveness of sin in our lives. Even our most upright actions are often tainted with sinful motives. Furthermore, referring to misbehavior as a sin brings to mind the notion of a punishment or debt that needs to be paid. The sacrifice of Jesus Christ on the cross serves as the payment for our sin. In a heart-centered classroom the consequence may be used to deter or to teach; it is not to be seen as a payment. Children and young people who are stuck in their sin need to be shown a way out. One who teaches through discipline, rather than reacts, shows where the current path is leading and graciously helps the student to change course.

Conclusion

Working with students who need to change takes patience. The quality of patience is not a trait found strictly in the chromosomes. It is a virtue learned through practicing what one believes about loving others. Heart-centered teachers cultivate patience in two forms. Immediate patience influences their first response to misbehavior. Stubborn patience guides their slow and steady work of affecting heart-felt change. It is patience in the long-term, a steadfast spirit that refuses to give up on kids.

It's time to take a closer look at the practical implications of stubborn patience in the classroom. How do teachers acquire that quality in the face of children or young people who come off as their enemies? What real differences should stubborn patience make among attitudes that stink? Finally, when misbehavior does not appear to be rooted in a detrimental attitude, what sort of measures keep pleasant students from turning sour? As I make suggestions in the chapters that follow, there is one concept about redirecting discipline that we must keep squarely in front of us. Heart-centered teachers avoid losing the battle with students because they choose to decline fighting in the first place. Teachers of the heart hold onto their teaching role in every situation.

Chapter 9:
Calm Authority

Anger and Fear

Anger is one emotion I have learned to manage in teaching. Like most people who've survived more than twenty years in a classroom full of adolescents, I am less perturbable today than when I began. Still, a disregard for authority can really stoke my coals, even now. One eruption occurred not long before I wrote this chapter. Three or four kids in the back of the room were pulling faces and laughing at each other while I was reviewing for a test. Then, just after I had stopped the lesson and told them to knock it off, I heard the snickers again and turned to see someone else's face in a contorted grimace. That was it. The marker in my hand slammed against the floor, and pieces of it went flying. Then I yelled at everybody for a couple of minutes.

Reacting like that was dumb and ineffective, considering the other options that were available. My real mistake, though, was not that I became angry. It was relinquishing control of my response. I "lost it." And in giving up that control, I wrecked more than just a marker. Despite all of the maturity I showed after that day, I was regarded as a crab by those who could not get past the marker scene. Six months later, some were still unable to fully trust me, reporting that the incident made them feel uncomfortable in my class.

The emotion of fear is even more disturbing, however, than anger. I feel threatened when students bring their defiance to a new level by taking others along with them. When students usurp my authority using the power they hold over their classmates, my self-confidence takes a hit. Though physical safety has never been an issue, I have felt out-matched by the kingpins in a class. I've had negative, anti-learning behaviors going on all around me and felt powerless to do anything about it.

Teachers can maintain a stronger sense of authority in the classroom by learning to keep the emotions of anger and fear within their proper confines. The art of nonverbal communication helps a person to stay calm while concurrently transmitting his or her authority to the group. One prominent figure in the field of nonverbal conveyance is Fred Jones.

I discovered one of his books early on in my teaching, when I was still searching for a decent classroom management "system." Its title, *Positive Classroom Discipline*, seemed a refreshing alternative to the negativity I had been grappling with.[1] Though the marker story proves that I wasn't completely transformed by Jones's advice, I have still learned a great deal from him.

Jones, whose background is in the field of psychology, describes the body language of "interpersonal power" in the context of the classroom. The way we carry ourselves around misbehaving students communicates far more about our "teacher presence" than the words we use or the threats we hold over them. Jones's system, which he calls "limit-setting," equips teachers to set the limits or boundaries of a classroom without getting drawn into battle. In a moment we are going to spend some time looking at Jones's strategies and related methods for maintaining one's authority among students as misbehaviors occur.

Objections to Power

Perhaps the word "power" in connection with teaching makes you uncomfortable. Teachers can and should use their authority to gain control in vexing situations, but their motives should never be self-serving, as the term "power" might suggest. Though Jones has toned down the emphasis on power in his more recent writings, he still insists that power is an unavoidable aspect of any social setting, including the classroom.[2]

The reason I am drawn to Jones's approach is that he does not promote a self-seeking or boisterous sense of power. The main objective in limit-setting is for teachers to remain calm so that they can calm the atmosphere, allowing misbehaving students opportunity to change their course without a showdown or embarrassment. According to Jones, "[r]eal interpersonal power is the power of calm in which room is left for both parties to retain their dignity and sense of volition—the door is constantly left open for affirmation and, if necessary, reconciliation."[3]

Another potential objection to Jones is that his limit-setting procedure is sometimes associated with Lee and Marlene Canter's assertive discipline program, which relies heavily on punishments and rewards. In view of the shortcomings of manipulative management techniques that we saw in Chapter Two, you might wonder why I would include Jones'

---

1 Jones, F. (1987). *Positive classroom discipline.* New York: McGraw-Hill, Inc.
2 Jones, F. (2007). *Tools for teaching.* Santa Cruz, California: Fredrick H. Jones & Associates, Inc.
3 Jones, Fredric. (1987). P. 86.

strategies in my repertoire. When students are unmotivated or resistant, shouldn't we first consider the root causes of their behavior and attempt to teach rather than coerce?

Yes, there are pitfalls in Jones's reasoning, from a heart-centered point of view. At the end of this chapter we will examine the drawbacks of his thinking, as well as any approach that prescribes a formula for discipline. If we are serious, though, about "stubborn patience," about redirecting instead of reacting, the concepts of nonverbal communication merit consideration. Teachers who come unglued or who fall to pieces when they are challenged will struggle to provide effective discipline of any sort, whether coercive or compassionate. By contrast, limit-setting and similar strategies enable reactive teachers to operate in more of a redirecting mode. When these strategies are practiced, the process also builds a sense of confidence and quietude that has a carry-over effect. Once both teacher and students realize that there is little a student can do to gain control over the teacher, it becomes easier for the teacher to implement the other kinds of heart-centered discipline strategies we will find in subsequent chapters. Whereas some teachers exhibit calm authority naturally, there are plenty of others (myself included) who have benefited from a little instruction.

The Basics of Limit-Setting

Let's start with three fundamentals. First, calm signals strength; upset signals weakness. Whether a teacher is upset out of anger or out of fear makes no difference. If you cannot manage your own emotions, students know that you cannot manage them. Second, calmness is achieved by behaving calmly. In other words, it is the outward display of self-possession that leads to internal calmness in the face of a challenge. If you can exude composure, you will settle both your students and your own insides, which is one of the primary conditions of limit-setting. Finally, how does a teacher respond calmly in the face of provocation? Ironically, by doing very little at all. This principle is usually the hardest for teachers to accept, at least in practice, because it contradicts an assumption that I've noticed in my own experience: when the going gets tough, the tough get gruff.

The Look

Most of us are familiar with "the look" as a silent warning for wayward students not to venture any further. Let's review this basic classroom management tool and expand its possibilities. We know that focusing the eyes on a disruptive student is sometimes enough to redirect her to her learning. If the disruption occurs during work time, however, while you are providing assistance to another individual, "the look" will accomplish more if you stop talking to the person you've been helping as you look at the disrupter. Cut your words off in the middle of a sentence instead of waiting for a natural break. Your sudden silence and steady gaze shows your commitment to addressing the problem, even though you have said nothing. The same goes for using "the look" during a whole-class lesson. If a student begins to disrupt while the teacher is addressing the group, the teacher can abruptly stop talking and look at the disrupter.

The rest of a teacher's body either reinforces or contradicts the message communicated by the eyes. If you want a student to know you are serious, turn and face the person squarely. Remaining even slightly turned to the side telegraphs the message that you are not totally serious. Remember to keep your hands still as well; fidgety hands indicate nervousness.

Beyond the eyes and body stance, your face and tone of voice are other indicators of calm authority. It is important for the face to remain expressionless during limit-setting. Shooting a glare or clenching the jaw not only makes you look crabby; it allows your students to think that they have the power to upset you. The ideal face to wear, then, is not one of anger but complete boredom. For the same reason, it is also important to take the edge out of your voice if you speak. An angry or upset tone signals that the students have you; the calm tone reveals that you are still in control.

The Wait

One criticism of limit-setting is the amount of waiting time that it requires. It is true that time commitment is key to the success of limit-setting. According to Jones, if a particular disruption deserves any of your attention, it merits all of your attention until the students stop misbehaving and get back to their learning. The reason disrupters require your full attention is a practical issue rather than theoretical, says Jones. To paraphrase, it is not possible to learn while you are goofing off. I'd like to add a theoretical comment here, though. Time commitment to discipline is itself another way of communicating, without words, your resolve to maintaining a positive learning atmosphere.

What is accomplished through waiting? There are benefits for both you and the student. Waiting supports the three basic principles of communicating assertiveness through body language: calmness signals strength, calmness is achieved by behaving calmly, and one behaves calmly by doing very little. If you feel upset, either nervous or angry, waiting for compliance is useful for calming your own nerves and considering your next move. It communicates to the student that you are in control of yourself and that you have some control over the situation. Further, your willingness to wait gives a student ample opportunity to comply without a showdown.

Whereas limit-setting appears to consume exorbitant time initially, the need for waiting usually dwindles as students learn about the teacher's commitment to addressing misbehavior. My experience is a case in point. Once students have picked up on the cues, a simple look in their direction is often enough to get them back to their learning.

The Motion

If the disruption does not stop, a teacher can use proximity. Walk at a slow, relaxed pace, focusing on the instigator. Stop in front of the student's desk and wait. At this point, most students become uncomfortable and stop the disruption. If the person hasn't complied after several seconds, the reason may be that he is looking back at you, wondering what you are going to do. Use a simple "prompt," calmly pointing to the paper on the desk or shifting your eyes from the student's face down to the assignment. The "prompt" tells the student that your goal is not to bully or to prove yourself; you merely want the person to start working again. If you want to know how a teacher should react in the case that proximity fails, you'll find plenty of advice in Jones' books. It's more likely, however, that the student will make some kind of remark to throw you off balance. We'll get to the issue of "backtalk" in a moment.

Proximity is a great strategy for extinguishing little problems before they grow. For example, simply standing by the desk of a student, while one continues to teach, is often enough to curb the disruption without detracting from the lesson. Unfortunately, the classroom arrangement can inhibit the process if it prevents a teacher from moving around quickly. For example, rows of desks, especially those that continue right up to a wall, block the teacher from circulating freely. Try to maintain open walkways so that you can nip budding problems nonchalantly—before they go to seed.

The Words

So far in the process, you've said little or nothing. How should you respond if the disrupter talks? To follow the limit-setting rules, you must treat any form of talk as "backtalk," though backtalk comes in many forms. One common type is defensive backtalk: *"What?"* or "Why are you looking at me?" The backtalk may appear innocent and take the form of a question, or the student may attempt to blame you for not explaining the lesson clearly: "I don't get this stuff," or "How are we supposed to do this? Some remarks, on the other hand, are direct attempts to provoke or upset. These comments typically refer to a teacher's personal hygiene, breath, or style of clothing. Then there is also nasty backtalk, which includes swearing.

Jones' guidance for backtalk is profoundly simple. All forms of backtalk have only one purpose: to change the teacher's agenda and get the student "off the hook." There are ways that you don't want to respond. In helping the misbehaving student who suddenly asks for assistance, you show that it is possible to get help by disrupting the class. In responding to a nasty remark, you open the door for a showdown. Focus then, not on what the student is saying but instead on what the student is attempting to do, namely, to throw you off course. One of the great ironies of limit-setting, remember, is that doing *next to nothing* can be the most effective way to communicate your authority.

If the student makes a comment after you've initiated limit-setting, do not respond with words. Check to make sure that your jaw is not clenched, and maintain the bored expression. Look at the person and wait. When the teacher shows no response to backtalk, most students eventually begin to feel awkward and run out of things to say. Wait calmly for a few seconds, then gently remind the child to return to the assignment with a prompt if you need to. But do so without intimidating. Your goal is not to "win;" you only want them to resume their learning.

Some students use inappropriate language to derail the teacher. If you react to an offensive word, their goal is accomplished. Of course bad language in the classroom is inexcusable and needs to be addressed. However, you still need to confront it on your own terms. Jones's advice is to proceed with limit-setting, as you would with any other form of backtalk. When the class ends, tell the student that you would like to talk. Doing so allows the person's classmates to see that you will not tolerate the sort of language that was used. Additionally, choosing to wait before confronting the student allows time for both of you to calm down and often makes for a more sincere and productive conversation.

Despite Jones's advice on swearing, my personal preference is to underscore the seriousness of bad language by holding the conversation immediately. Stopping class for a moment and calmly asking a student to step into the hallway sends a message to the student—and everyone else—that certain lines are not worth crossing. If I feel that I can remain cool-headed enough, addressing profanity on the spot would be my choice over waiting.

Why should a teacher remain calm in the face of offensive language? Your election to remain unruffled when the event occurs enables the student to save face in front of her peers. The person lashed out at you with words, yet you held your ground and even responded with gentleness. Why is it important to "protect" the very student who has tried to upset you? Your calmness retains your authority in the classroom, and it is pivotal for the direction of your conversation with the student outside the classroom. In the next chapter we will look more closely at guidelines for personal confrontations.

Beyond Limit-Setting

Jones' advice for asserting authority with calmness is astonishingly practical. After more than two decades of using it, I am still amazed by how well it works. In this short chapter, however, it would be neither possible nor appropriate to replicate all of the particulars of limit-setting, such as the timing of certain responses or training one's body to relax. A number of these seemingly small details often appear to make or break the results. A person wishing to give Jones's ideas a serious try should read directly from his materials or enroll in a seminar. Jones himself admits, however, that there are also limits to limit-setting. He includes additional strategies for situations when teachers must abandon limit-setting, valuable information for anyone who desires more specifics.

As professionals, teachers who develop a skill eventually learn to apply the basics of the technique in different kinds of situations without strictly adhering to each step of the procedure. When I move beyond limit-setting—by choosing to speak to the students instead of waiting, for instance—I still find that the fundamentals of limit-setting increase the effectiveness of any classroom confrontation.

For one, when a teacher begins to feel upset or angry in the classroom, an economy of words is often best. Shortness of speech minimizes the chance that students will pick up on the anxiety or the exasperation you feel and believe that they have gained some sort of power over you. Even if justifiably angry, conciseness prevents the incident from stealing too much attention away from the learning or from making the situation about you, the teacher.

In addition, a short statement combined with "the look" I referred to earlier can also put an end to problems before they escalate. For example, sometimes students will come to each other's aid during a confrontation in the classroom. If someone is able to get others laughing while the teacher is feeling rattled, one response that often works is to speak to the "heckler" but focus your eyes on the others. In a voice just loud enough for everyone to hear, say, "*I* didn't think that was very funny." The success of this response, as I mentioned, seems to lie in looking *not at the student who made the remark*, but at another individual who is laughing. "Lock in" your gaze until that person stops giggling, then look at several others, each in turn, until the room is silent. Having said it, wait a little longer before continuing the lesson.

The inactivity and self-composure of a person in the midst of situations where students are used to seeing teachers tense up or blow up is sometimes enough to generate its own ripple of nervous laughter in the room. This reaction is not to be seen as a threat. The tittering is a natural response to the sheer oddity of a teacher maintaining control in such a calm manner. Take it as a sort of "nonverbal" compliment, but don't gloat or you'll ruin everything. As smoothly as possible, refocus the students on their learning.

Creating a distraction is another technique that can offset antagonism in the classroom. If you feel that the students are trying to get you upset and no other response has worked so far, try fighting the distraction with a distraction of your own. What sort of diversion is at your disposal in the middle of a showdown? Almost anything having to do with the lesson, naturally! In any classroom intervention, a teacher needs to remember that the ultimate question is not "Who's the boss?" but rather "What are we here to accomplish today?" Skillfully shifting everyone's focus back to the learning not only neutralizes the toxic vapor in the air, it redirects students to what they ought to be doing in the first place. The key to success here lies partly in the subtlety. "Justin and Sheri, get back to *work!*" is a command, and as such, it depends on the speaker's authority which is the very thing in question at the moment. Pointing to an object, asking a question, or directing a student to explain something related to the lesson are just a few ways teachers can bring a new and neutral thought to the forefront of the class's collective mind. The problem that led to the face-off during class can still be dealt with after class, when the teacher and the instigator have calmed down and are able to speak to each other without the interference of an audience.

A common mistake with the distraction strategy, however, especially among beginning teachers, is to continue teaching while ignoring a student who continues to disrupt. Turning a blind eye to a problem, in the hope that it will go away, sends the message that a teacher is neither serious about the lesson or about addressing those who would detract from it. If the "distraction maneuver" fails, it may be time to confront the student outside in the hallway, away from the audience in the classroom.

If it becomes necessary to resort to anger in the classroom, remember to "*use* it; don't *lose* it," and then to reestablish a sense of calmness as quickly as possible. When I threw the marker in class, anger itself was not the problem. My mistake was losing control of myself—acting like a fathead. The mistake diminished my authority. Those who caused the problem suddenly realized how easily they could gain the upper hand on me, while the more timid students in the class did not feel that they could trust me.

Recall that in "reactive discipline," emotions control the response; in "redirecting discipline," the mind controls the response. The main objective in using anger in the classroom is to get the attention of those who haven't clued in to the seriousness of their error and then to get them back on track with their learning. Teachers can appropriately gain that attention by momentarily raising their voice, for example. Once students have recognized that the teacher means business, the person's voice can return to a more natural volume.

Keep in mind, though, that anger is not the only way to regain students' attention. Consequences that address the behavior may also be a viable option. For instance, I could have required the offenders to meet with me for a special study session over lunch since they weren't using class time to review. In levying a consequence—instead of merely venting—I would have allowed the offenders to experience the discomfort of their own bad choices instead of taking all of that discomfort upon myself.

Problems with Packaged Plans

While Fred Jones has trained thousands of teachers to let their minds rather than their emotions guide them, I would caution against adopting his entire philosophy of classroom management. Here are a few assumptions to question, not only in Jones but in many who "package" a management style.

Though limit-setting is useful for establishing one's authority in the classroom, we have to remember where the ultimate authority lies. In one sense, limit-setting could be viewed as a way to push one's weight around. As some have complained, Jones's techniques are just a form of intimidation. We've already discussed the snags of intimidation and other forms of manipulation. Those who want their students to grow into responsible and caring persons, as opposed to people who merely avoid punishment, must learn to think beyond the immediate situation. Submitting to the authority of God, a heart-centered teacher would exercise an attitude of humility, even while redirecting wayward students. Keeping in mind the climate of the classroom, and the attitudes that this climate seeks to grow, a teacher would remember that limit-setting is one tool in an entire repertoire, to be used only when it serves the best interests of the students. It helps to keep in mind the purpose of limit-setting: the responsibility we have as teachers to both maintain a learning environment and to help students develop their own self-control.

Another popular theme among those who sell techniques for child rearing is an over reliance on consistency, and Jones is no exception. The common assumption is that any management system will fall apart without clear and indisputable boundaries. Jones reasons that there is no such thing as *mostly* consistent. He argues that in being consistent *most of the time* (but not *all* of the time), parents and teachers "turn children into brats."

On the one hand, a teacher does have to create a climate where students respect the rules—handing things in on time, listening while someone else speaks, working quietly during study time so that others can concentrate, and so on. An authority figure who states boundaries without enforcing them invites frustration and chaos. Yet, the issue is a little more complex than being 100 percent consistent.

A teacher who mutes anyone who talks out of turn smothers insightful comments and ideas before they take their first breath. One who assumes that anybody who talks to another during work time is either creating a disruption or helping someone cheat squelches opportunities for students to care for each other in their learning. If consistency and follow-through *always* have precedence, respectfulness and learning will take a back seat.

The capstone of a heart-centered classroom is a climate where students respect each other and where learning is valued. Genuine respect, as we saw in Chapter Five, is about more than merely restraining oneself from hurting or bothering others. It includes going out of the way to help one's neighbor. Learning involves more than "on-task behavior." Meaningful learning includes sharing, questioning, and debating—and yes, sometimes even talking out of turn.

We must further note that grace also supersedes consistency. We saw this reality in Chapter Seven, in the discussion of reacting versus redirecting. In situations where a recalcitrant attitude drives a pattern of behavior, the ultimate goal lies beyond getting the misbehavior to desist. Our challenge is to address what lies beneath the surface of the problem and to look for ways to draw the person back. Sometimes a measure of grace accomplishes that goal better than rigid compliance to the discipline system.

When choosing or evaluating a classroom discipline plan, a teacher seeking a heart-centered climate would ask questions that relate to the guidelines for redirecting. Does the response merely put a stop to wrong behavior, for example, or does it encourage right behavior? Do the measures address the past but also move students beyond? Do wayward children or young people have any opportunity to think about the natural consequences of their actions? Does the plan allow a teacher to consider possible reasons for misbehavior and adjust accordingly? How do teachers retain their authority while also caring for their students?

Conclusion

Gentleness and firmness do not always appreciate the other's company. When one of them appears in the doorway, the other usually heads for the fire escape. If a heart-centered approach to discipline is to have any effect, however, those two mismatched partners must learn to live with each other.

"Limit-setting" offers a practical way to intervene gently but firmly, especially when students attempt to challenge a teacher's authority. Teachers seeking to establish a heart-centered classroom climate, however, are careful to keep their authority in proper perspective. They also consider the larger situation before choosing the most appropriate response. Let's take a look next at personal confrontations in the context of a heart-centered atmosphere. How should we talk with students about their behavior and about the attitudes that drive their behavior?

CHAPTER 10:
ONE TO ONE

Cows and Bullies

Growing up on a farm in southern Iowa, whenever we turned our cattle loose into a new pasture, we noticed that certain ones always had to check the boundaries before they were content to do anything else. Of course some were appropriately happy to settle in at first sight of their summer estate: rolling hills with all-you-can-eat greens undulating in the light air, a welcoming tree-lined creek on the east fringe, and a stunning view of contoured corn rows in the adjacent field to the south. Those cows knew they were in clover, and they were grateful. By contrast, the restless ones in the herd would immediately form a group and walk the entire fence line, taking stock of their confines.

My dad, who liked to point out this phenomenon, also remarked that you'd rarely see any cows get shocked as they marched along that wire. Somehow they could sniff out the electricity in the air and stay just far enough away to avoid the jolt. In addition, after finding where the boundaries lay, the cows would continue to test the line for as long as the pasture was their home. If anything caused the fence to short out, it

didn't take long for a leader to discover the breach and invite the rest of the herd to a party in the neighbor's cornfield.

Do you see the parallel between human nature and the nature of cattle? There lives within most of us a propensity to test the boundaries. We like to know what our limits are. In Chapter Nine we saw that teachers who remain calm amid "boundary pushers" in the classroom minimize the effects of contrary attitudes. However, if teachers want to grow *new* attitudes, they also look for opportunities to talk with wayward children one-to-one, outside the classroom setting.

The urge to become nervous or angry in the whole-class setting is natural because a teacher works among spectators. Anyone in the "crowd" could potentially come to the aid of the student under discipline. Furthermore, a teacher's response in class is always under scrutiny. Even if onlookers remain passive during a discipline event, one can be sure that those students are taking note of where the boundaries lie and how strong they are.

In one-to-one confrontations, where odds are stacked more in favor of the teacher, we must resist an urge to strong-arm the wayward student. Teachers who use the one-to-one confrontation to bully wayward children inadvertently miss two goals of heart-centered confrontations.

Two Intents; Not Too Intense

Two objectives would take precedence in a heart-centered confrontation. The first is leading students to accept responsibility for their behavior instead of predisposing them to deny a problem or to blame others or circumstances. The second goal is to offer a new vision. When students' actions stem from the way they see things, inviting them to look at things differently is a natural solution.

Unfortunately, difficult students are not always inclined to accept responsibility or to view the world from someone else's perspective. Their own way of seeing and responding makes more sense to them, or they build up walls around themselves to keep others from evoking change. We have already noted that only the Holy Spirit can generate change from the inside out. However, our words and the tones that carry them can either get in the way of the Spirit's work or encourage it.[1] As we look at the principles of heart-centered confrontations, we have to consider what factors would soften a person's outer shell and what factors would serve, in effect, to toughen it.

As you might guess, gaining a student's trust is a crucial first step in

---

1   Van Dyk, J. (2005). *The craft of Christian teaching*. Sioux Center, Iowa: Dordt Press.

attending to the heart, and it's a process that needs to begin before the first reprimand. What happens aside from any confrontation is every bit as important, then, as what happens during a confrontation. Some of the suggestions offered in this chapter would make little sense apart from the context of a heart-centered atmosphere that we have already examined. The time you spend listening to your students and talking with them in your daily activities builds their trust and provides valuable insight about the factors that influence their behavior. Your consistency and fairness add to the trust your students place in you. Your willingness to admit a mistake and to apologize sincerely not only models an appropriate way to respond to reproach, but also further strengthens the trust that is needed for heart-centered confrontations.

In Chapter Four, I left a loose end that needs to be tied up now. We were discussing the issue of self-esteem and its relevance to a heart-centered classroom climate. The question raised before we left that topic referred to self-esteem and discipline: how does self-esteem factor in when contriteness of heart is key to a change of heart?

The pain of seeing our wrong is actually a gift if it sends us running to the forgiving arms of our Savior and produces a genuine change in our hearts and in our actions. What teacher demeanor nudges a student toward healthy remorse? Tactics like humiliation, embarrassment, intimidation, preaching, and biting sarcasm lead students in the opposite direction. Remember from our earlier discussion that when the "self" is under attack, protecting oneself usually takes precedence over seeing the bigger picture or comprehending the natural consequences of one's actions. A confrontation that attacks or belittles someone encourages that person to become defensive or to shift the blame.

Sometimes the actions of students do merit an appropriate tongue-lashing. Just don't expect those persons to own up to their mistakes, however, if you stay angry the whole time you talk to them. It's a matter of pragmatics rather than philosophy: students under verbal assault will usually look for a way to save face, if not during the confrontation, then possibly afterwards in the way they speak of you to others. Is a "tough approach" incompatible with heart-centered discipline then? No; as we will see in a moment, a heart-centered teacher is as tough as he or she needs to be. The consequences a teacher imposes, for example, when those consequences are merited, may feel appropriately tough or unpleasant from a student's perspective. But during a confrontation itself, when a teacher is trying to get a student to come to grips with his behavior, gentleness usually wins over heavy-duty.

It would be impossible for me to dictate a proper way to confront someone. Your students are different from mine, and they are also different from each other. Their personalities, their personal histories, and their motives all influence the choices that they make. All of these factors call for different approaches. The styles of confrontations heart-centered teachers employ cover a spectrum from gentle to coercive, as seen in the two lists below:

Gentle	Coercive
Empathetic tone	Objective tone
Occasionally lighthearted approach	No-nonsense approach
Two-way conversation	One-way conversation
Focused on effects of behavior	Focused on rules
Natural consequences	Levied consequences

Let me be clear that gentle and coercive are not to be seen as opposites, or as either-or choices. Heart-centered teachers always discipline within the context of grace, graciously allowing students to be free of their guilt but also guiding them away from their wrongful paths.

Based on earlier discussions, we know that we can usually accomplish more by tending toward the gentle side. In addition, within a heart-centered classroom climate we have more opportunities to use gentleness in confrontations. That sort of climate, you see, extends the possibilities of gentle tactics to students and situations that would require a more coercive approach in a manipulative classroom atmosphere. Yet because some children and young people lack the understanding, the maturity, or the cooperative spirit necessary for purely gentle discipline, coercion is still unavoidable—even in heart-centered classrooms.

Coercive discipline can be carried out with compassion, though. Which teacher appears to be the most compassionate: the one who gets huffy and issues threats without follow-through, or the one who remains calm but levies an appropriate consequence? An electric fence for cattle doesn't make noise; the deterrent is in the pain of pushing up against it. Teachers who attempt to grow a new attitude through the use of coercion optimize their chances for success when they find ways to encourage and support the student despite the discomfort of the consequences those students may have earned. One can intensify the penalty, when necessary, without intensifying one's tone. Anger may serve as the opening, but it must not have the final word. Heart-centered confrontations end by pointing students ahead instead of stopping them where they are.

The relaxed physical demeanor has a dual effect: it puts the nervous child at ease, but it also keeps resistant students from manipulating the situation. Young people used to having their way with adults who become upset find that it is difficult to take advantage of a teacher who listens carefully and waits to respond. Teachers who get agitated or who react too quickly sometimes deny students the opportunity to come to terms with their own wrongfulness.

To summarize, a heart-centered confrontation serves two intents or purposes: to encourage students to take responsibility for their behavior and to offer a new way of perceiving, a new way of acting. A teacher expands the likelihood of meeting those goals by reducing the intensity of the dialogue.

Shifting a Course

Though healthy confrontations vary in length and complexity, most typically include three steps or phases: opening the conversation by stating the problem, listening to the student's perspective if he or she is willing to share it, and responding. As I lay out the guidelines for implementing each step within a heart-centered framework, we will also follow a story that concurs with the explanation of each phase. The narrative will be shared in three parts, each section coming directly after the step it exemplifies.

Opening

In raising the issue, the teacher focuses more on observations and less on impressions or interpretations. "You've been disrespectful," for instance, is an interpretation of the student's actions or words. Though this interpretation *may* be correct, the teacher really hasn't yet proven that the behavior was intended in this way. The student, who probably feels judged by the statement would now likely look for an escape by denying ("No, I haven't been."), faking ignorance ("Huh?"), minimizing ("Whatever!"), or by repelling ("That's *your* problem").

Difficult students use escape tactics to shift responsibility for a problem back to the teacher who must now defend her claim with evidence or enter a power play in the hope of intimidating the student into confessing. Furthermore, if the accusation was unfair or misplaced, the teacher has broken a trust that will need to be repaired. Once again, a teacher aiming to get the student to accept responsibility would usually center this initial part of the confrontation around the behaviors observed. If necessary, one would then lead up to the impressions or the effects of those tactics. Let's watch for a moment now as Mr. Lee confronts Jason on his classroom behavior in freshman Algebra. Note the teacher's focus on Jason's actual deeds and not his seemingly disrespectful attitude.

At the sound of the bell, the students begin to gather up their things. Mr. Lee slips into an open desk next to Jason's and calmly gets his attention. "I need to talk with you for a moment, Jason."

"What is it *this* time?" Jason mutters. Avoiding eye contact with the teacher, Jason focuses on his books and pencils as he transfers them from the desk to his backpack.

"When students disrupt class, it makes teaching a lot more difficult for me."

"What are you yelling at *me* for? I didn't do nothing."

"Actually, I'm not yelling," Mr. Lee replies. His voice remains low and steady. "Three times in my class today, you took attention away from the lesson. First, you let your book slam to the floor. Later you blurted, 'What's for lunch?' Then, while I was showing how to solve a problem, you caused your neighbors to laugh. It's really hard for me to regain everyone's concentration when you do those kinds of things."

Listening

Whereas teachers may appropriately ask clarifying questions during the listening phase, questions that lead to defensiveness should be avoided. The rhetorical question, for instance, is really a statement posing as a question. When a teacher asks, "What were you thinking when you did that?" the accused may hear it as, "What kind of bovine *are* you?" Make no mistake: the problem is not always the wording of the question. It's the demeanor and the tone of voice that turn a question into an assertion and send the student looking for a way out. The incriminating question, a cousin of the rhetorical question, is asked by a teacher looking for an opportunity to pounce on the student. Teachers who voice incriminating questions are quick to interrupt the child by pointing out errors or perceived falsehoods. Once again, students who read the true intentions of questions like these tend to look for an escape rather than acknowledging their wrong.

Because heart-centered discipline seeks to shift an attitude rather than gain the upper hand, one must hear the individual as a person, as one who behaves according to a unique way of seeing things, as one whose emotions are real. A student's perception may not match reality, but for the moment her perceptions are reality to her. This view does not leave the child stuck in her (perhaps) misguided point of view; it merely recognizes that if an attitude is to change, one must begin where the student is. If the student is willing to share her perspective on the problem, the heart-centered teacher will tune in not only to the surface details but also to what lies beneath. Before responding, the teacher would also first acknowledge that the student's point has been heard. Summarizing the student's comments or simply waiting a moment before speaking shows that the listener has taken everything in.

What about the student who lies? Those who attempt to cover up the truth often talk themselves into a corner, especially when an attentive teacher poses the right questions. Exposing inconsistencies within the story or sharing points where the story diverges from the teacher's observations can also bring the truth to light. When it's not possible to prove dishonesty, a teacher may choose to let the matter rest for awhile. A person's heart usually reveals itself over time through patterns of behavior rather than a single incident. A teacher who gives a listening ear to even the deceptive student will, in the long term, find more opportunities to work with that student's attitude than the teacher who verbally lunges at a person every time a falsehood is detected. Let's return now to the story of Mr. Lee and Jason, picking up just after Mr. Lee makes his statement about students laughing.

"I didn't make anybody laugh at me, Jason argues." Even though the snickers had come from Jason's part of the room, Mr. Lee knows that he cannot prove his allegation. During class, students were giggling while the teacher had taken a moment to write on the board. In the short time it took for him to turn back again, all of them had managed to refocus their eyes to the front of the classroom. Still, Mr. Lee was careful not to let Jason off the hook so easily. "Why were the students near you laughing?"

"*I* don't know!"

Mr. Lee remained quiet for a few seconds after this response. For now he would let the matter rest, yet the teacher's silence conveyed that he does not fully trust Jason's response. "Well, back to dropping your book on the floor..."

"It was an accident," Jason snapped. Finding it hard to stay calm now, Mr. Lee works to regain control of his nerves by drawing a slow breath and letting it out again.

"If it were an accident, I would have expected you to look surprised and maybe offer a short apology for the noise. Instead you smiled at the kids sitting next to you and took your time retrieving the book."

Mr. Lee waited a moment for Jason to reply, but Jason stayed quiet, his eyes on his book bag. "Finally, why would you need to interrupt me in class to ask about lunch when the menu is available on-line weeks in advance?"

"I don't know," Jason shrugged. "Hungry, I guess." Jason glanced at the clock. Students in the next class were beginning to enter, and Mr. Lee knew they had run out of time.

"Well, Jason, we will need to finish our conversation later. Tomorrow before homeroom, I need you to stop by my room. For now you'd better get to your next class. See you in the morning." Mr. Lee was not disappointed about postponing the end of the confrontation. He needed time to consider the best response, and he suspected that Jason would be doing a little contemplating of his own. Sometimes the anxiety in waiting to find out what the teacher will do brings about more soul-searching and regret than the actual consequence.

<u>Responding</u>

Whether the teacher chooses a response that is more gentle or more coercive, one fundamental of heart-centered discipline pervades. Recall from Chapter Eight on "Stubborn Patience" the paradigm shift of seeing behavior problems as learning problems. Those who treat misbehavior as a learning issue employ a teaching style in their confrontations with students, while adults who reduce misbehavior to wickedness opt for preaching. (Sermons, of course, play a vital role in the lives of believers. My reference here is not to the helpful aspects of preaching but to the bullying connotation of the word.)

In the classroom, effective teachers show that something is true rather than merely declare it. Heart-centered teachers strive to do the same in their confrontations, helping the student see how the action has caused hurt or showing where the student's current path is leading. Effective teachers also understand the importance of the personal struggle in acquiring knowledge and skills. Instead of spoon-feeding information, they often choose instead to provide clues, leading students to find the solution or grasp the concept. In a heart-centered confrontation, a teacher also would use no more words than necessary to get the point across.

If a teacher wants the student to take responsibility, one might also ask the student about what could be done to set things right. Whereas this question is unlikely to produce a genuine answer in a confrontation where a student feels bullied or preached to, there is more potential in a setting where the student trusts the teacher and where the teacher has effectively helped the student to understand the consequences of the behavior.

A recalcitrant student, of course, may still resist the question or feign obliviousness to your concern. The "ignorance maneuver" at this point in the confrontation is often enough to push the blood pressure of the most forbearing person into the red zone. Stubborn patience reminds us, however, that attitudes do not change quickly. A confrontation is not necessarily a flop if the student fails to show remorse or make a sincere apology. Only the Holy Spirit can generate sincere repentance (which carries beyond feeling sorry to a change in behavior). As any effective teacher knows, students who struggle with new concepts or skills often don't "get it" after a couple, or even several, attempts. You may still give a consequence of your choice—and make it appropriately unpleasant, but showing your exasperation is likely to be counterproductive. If there is anything the child has to "learn," it may be that you will not be emotionally manipulated by anyone's tricks and that you do not give up that easily.

Heart-centered confrontations typically end on an encouraging note. Teachers who react, it seems, always look for the wrong in a person's attitude and try to stomp it out. Redirecting teachers, on the other hand, relentlessly look for something good that they can fan into flame. Regardless of the route one takes in a confrontation, gentle or coercive, a teacher would find a way to close by pointing the student ahead. This type of "send-off" finds the grace to focus on the future instead of dwelling in the past. Let's return one more time to Mr. Lee and Jason as they finish their conversation in the morning.

"Thanks for coming in Jason. Please have a seat."

"Jason, what were the things you did yesterday that I had to talk with you about?"

"I dropped my book on the floor and asked what was for lunch."

"Yes; thanks. And how about the part where students were laughing?"

Jason waits a moment before responding. "Well, it might have been me."

"Do you understand why students shouldn't draw negative attention to themselves in class?

"Yeah, it's hard for you to teach. But algebra is so *boring* sometimes. And your examples don't make any sense to me."

"I know algebra isn't your favorite subject, Jason. If you have ideas on how to make the class more meaningful, I'd be happy to hear them. Also, if you need some extra help before our test next week, I would enjoy working with you. Believe it or not, I like doing the things we learn about in algebra! But, Jason, to express your boredom by drawing attention to yourself is disrespectful, and I can't allow it."

For the first time in the conversation, Jason looks at his teacher but remains silent. Mr. Lee continues: "Do I need to do anything to help you remember what we've talked about, or can you fix the problem of disrupting on your own?"

"I guess I can fix it on my own."

"Okay, good. Can you offer me any suggestions for improving my class?"

"Not right now, I guess."

"All right, then. One final question: "Could I help you with solving equations before next week?"

"Maybe. I'll see if I can get it first."

"Thanks, Jason. See you in class today."

Conclusion

A heart-centered confrontation strives for the two goals of leading a student to accept responsibly for behavior and helping that person to see differently. A change in perspective often leads to a change in behavior. Whereas personal confrontations may be gentle or coercive, a teacher can usually accomplish more through a compassionate approach.

Clearly, it is futile to prescribe a formula for personal confrontations that would apply to every person and circumstance. Yet, a heart-centered confrontation would apply certain principles in most situations. Foundationally, classroom climate and a factor of trust are crucial if a teacher wants the student to be honest. While confronting, a teacher would focus on observations rather than on impressions and listen instead of interrupting or asking accusatory questions. In responding, heart-centered teachers retain their role as teachers, showing rather than declaring. Even if an imposed consequence is warranted, they levy it in a way that redirects rather than reacts. Finally, that quality of stubborn patience accepts the reality that attitudes do not typically change during one meeting with a student. Sometimes the most we can do is to provide consistency and a context in which the Holy Spirit can work.

Now that we have discussed addressing misbehaviors on a personal level, let's look at some ideas for addressing behavior concerns that involve multiple students.

CHAPTER 11:
UPROOTING UNKINDNESS

Dealing With Dynamics

During my second year of teaching, the jocks in the class would sometimes stand on either side of our classroom door and quietly make comments to each other about the girls who walked through.

Even though I sensed that the girls felt degraded by this pastime, I don't know exactly why I never told those guys to find something else to do. The "reviews" usually occurred in the morning as the students were arriving, so perhaps my need to be ready for the day seemed more urgent than the call to get involved in student affairs. You had to have your ducks in a row with these kids, and walking across the room for a confrontation would have consumed costly prep time.

On the other hand, maybe I just didn't know what to say. I hadn't invested a lot of time in getting to know this group of boys, so confronting them was never much fun. They realized the strength in numbers and often argued with me when they were together. How would I respond if Joshua rolled his eyes and groaned or if Micah turned and muttered something to Matthew? Technically, they weren't breaking any rules; it was quiet in the room, and their homework was ready. None of the girls ever walked away crying, so the matter probably wasn't worth my trouble.

Neither of those two reasons makes any sense to me now. Adequate preparation is still a must, but I can't just stay at my desk if I know that someone is getting hurt or humiliated.[1] Splitting up little rings of troublemakers doesn't bother me the way it used to, either. It's almost as satisfying as breaking the rack in a game of pool. Unfortunately, my students rarely give me that kind of opportunity anymore. After they figure out that I won't put up with harassment, those who want to make others miserable find more furtive outlets for their unkindness.

This type of conflict is one of the most challenging aspects of classroom discipline. I refer to it as negative classroom dynamics. A negative

---

1   It goes without saying that if a teacher wants to prevent problems as students mingle about the room, the chair behind one's desk probably isn't the most strategic vantage point. The time before class begins provides an opportunity both for building relationships with students and for discovering tensions that need addressing.

–117–

classroom dynamic is any sort of noxious influence that multiplies and preys on the relationships in a group. Generally speaking, conflict reaches "dynamic" proportions only when a disagreeable frame of mind affects large numbers of students. While problems that are limited to one individual or to a small subset within a class may morph into patterns that affect the entire group, an isolated tension that can be handled in a one-to-one confrontation is not considered a classroom dynamic. An issue rises to that level only if the virus proliferates.

As mentioned a moment ago, a negative classroom dynamic breaks down relationships. It may pit students against other students or create tension between students and teachers. In heart-centered classrooms, where a great deal of teaching depends upon trusting relationships, a negative dynamic can become a major obstacle. It saps motivation and cooperation. Students with questions keep their curiosity inside; they avoid thinking creatively and shy away from taking risks.

Resisting a negative dynamic is exhausting because the thing you're grappling with remains so elusive. The problem is not just the misbehaviors, the remarks, or the body language; it is what drives all of those things. Tighter boundaries and stiffer consequences are a logical and common response to the symptoms of negative dynamics: "These kids need to know where the lines are, and somebody's got to hold them accountable for their choices." Whereas firmness and logical consequences are often a necessary part of the solution, a teacher must concurrently work on creating the collaborative atmosphere of a learning community, as we discussed in Chapters Five and Six. Eradicating a negative classroom dynamic through reactive measures alone is like fighting dandelions with a flyswatter.

Because the two areas of negative classroom dynamics (student-versus-student and student-versus-teacher) encompass such a wide array of problems and potential solutions, this chapter will address only conflict among students while the next will deal with conflict between students and teachers.

Diagnose Before Treating

How should a teacher respond when students provoke each other? The reactive approach follows a more traditional view: give the kids what they've got coming to them. Unfortunately, meting out punishments only addresses part of the problem. Whereas justice may be served when troublemakers pay their due, a "payback mentality" reinforces the idea that one ill-treatment deserves another. Furthermore, a traditional response fails to repair a sense of community, which usually suffers in a conflict. The teacher (or principal) levies a consequence on the offender, but the victim and the offender remain at odds.

A redemptive approach would tend more toward the concept of restorative justice, where troublemakers are asked to consider the natural consequences of their actions—the damage they have caused. Victims are also included in the process with an opportunity to express their hurt directly to the offender and to share what they believe would set things right. Restorative justice requires culprits to restore what they have broken, but it also seeks to restore the culprits themselves: those hurt are asked to forgive the ones who have wronged them.[2]

Whereas restorative justice corresponds well with heart-centered discipline, this approach also has limits. Not every conflict is momentous enough to call for that kind of attention. Also, in some conflicts the offenders and the victims are not always easy to sort out. Finally, restorative justice may fall short where the instigator lacks an ability to comprehend the feelings of another or when personal safety is in jeopardy. The greater need is an entire approach to discipline that restores, regardless of the response that is chosen. Before responding to conflict, then, heart-centered teachers consider the nature of the problem and the possible intentions of those involved. In addition, teachers consider how their response will affect the community of the classroom.

Before the Climate Goes South

An isolated incident of rudeness or inconsideration is small in comparison to fighting or bullying, and drawing negative attention to a minor problem, unfortunately, runs the risk of amplifying that problem. Yet regardless of how small the incident may seem, rude or inconsiderate behavior cannot coexist with a classroom climate that fosters community. And again, minor problems can expand into tensions that affect the entire group. So any seemingly trivial situation that arises should still be addressed, albeit with caution.

A large degree of building or repairing a positive classroom atmosphere involves day-to-day reminders about how to function in a social setting, and sometimes the best response to an isolated incident is just that—a simple reminder. A teacher can "tweak" the way students interact with each other without conducting a major overhaul, and one who enjoys a good rapport with students can often pull it off with a smile or

---

2   For an excellent collection of articles devoted to the concept of restorative justice in schools, see *Christian Educators Journal.* October, 2010. Volume 50, No 1.

even a smidgeon of humor.

"Kari, is *that* the way you talk to your classmates?"

"Nolan, try asking her again, with a 'please.'"

"Fifth graders, it's pretty tough for someone to reason through a problem on the board when your classmates are snorting about the mistake you've just made."

A stern reaction to inconsiderate behavior only teaches students to control their rudeness when a teacher is present. The idea is not to communicate that the person in the wrong has been *bad*, but simply that this sort of speaking or behaving is unkind.

Responding to Nonverbal Jabs

When Brian hears Mr. Bouwkamp announce the name of his partner for a classroom assignment, he rolls his eyes. Then he gathers his things and slogs over to Michael's desk while some of the other students glance at each other and smirk. Over in the cafeteria at lunch break, while Mrs. Lief is cleaning up a spill, she notices six girls abruptly stand up and take their trays to a new table, leaving three behind at the original table. Just after lunch break, Jacob contorts his face in scorn as Bella walks by his locker. He looks at Carlos and Seth, who burst out laughing and shake their heads. After they finish gathering their things, they walk toward the classroom of Mr. Oudman who had witnessed their malicious behavior from his doorway.

Though nonverbal and nonphysical aggression can cause significant hurt, it's difficult to create rules and specific consequences for addressing it. Part of the problem is that the most destructive element is not the behavior itself but the attitude underneath the behavior, a creature too slippery to be caught with mere consequences. Given the fact that attitudes often originate from a perspective—a way of seeing, the best solution is to provide a new perspective. Sometimes the teacher must take the initiative to provide that perspective. In the three cases just mentioned, for example, it is unlikely that any of the injured parties would ask for intervention, especially if they are older. To do so would add to the humiliation they already feel.

"Straight talk" is a response that exposes not just the inappropriateness of the behavior but the probable feelings of the victim. Straight talk is matter-of-fact rather than preachy, and it does not belabor a point. If it is done well, those in the wrong feel a twinge of guilt and rightly so. Those who were treated unkindly are validated and hopefully spared future embarrassment. Straight talk also establishes the teacher as a person who cares about the ways students treat each other and who stands ready to protect students from hurt.

Straight talk can be used in a personal confrontation, obviously, because in some cases a personal confrontation is the best way to handle negative body language. Bella, for example, should be spared any undue attention in the injustice she received. Because Mr. Oudman is a sensitive teacher, he delays the three young men before they enter his classroom.

Unfortunately, a single personal confrontation isn't always possible. Mrs. Lief, who saw the group of girls "relocate" in the cafeteria, was tied up with another problem at the moment. By the time she could approach their table, the bell had rung and she wouldn't see the girls again until they came to her English class that afternoon. Brian's treatment of Michael involved several students in the classroom, so this problem would need to be addressed either with several personal confrontations or a short talk in the whole-class setting.

In addressing problems that occur in a large-group setting with multiple offenders, a teacher needs to avoid adding to the embarrassment of the injured party. A teacher of younger children might look for an opportunity to address the group by sending the victim on a short errand, for instance. However, Mr. Bouwkamp knows that if Michael were asked to leave, he would probably sense the teacher's motive and feel even more alienated from his peers. Since this problem happened just before the students split into groups, Mr. Bouwkamp waits until the students have begun their assignment. Then he stops and talks with the individuals who reacted when the two boys' names were called. He also makes a point of addressing Brian while he and Michael are together. Michael's feelings are validated, and Brian has the opportunity to make amends without the concern of saving face in front of his classmates.

If the situation does not present an opportunity for an individual confrontation, a teacher should address the group with a succinct and unvarnished statement. "Let's be careful to act in ways that build others up." The statement could be punctuated with a notable pause, during which the teacher would look at Brian and several of the others for a moment before resuming the lesson.

While a teacher should make a one-to-one confrontation with the primary offender soon after an event occurs, belaboring the point any more in the whole-class setting is usually unnecessary and detrimental. Sermonizing, though tempting, draws undue attention to the problem and seems to add momentum to a negative dynamic. In the case of Michael and his classmates, Mr. Bouwkamp would want to dismantle that dynamic and replace it with a healthier one. This transformation is a process that takes time, as we have already noted, and since dynamics rarely occur in a vacuum, the teacher has work to do in various places. Perhaps there is a reason students do not like working with Michael. Mr. Bouwkamp makes a note to investigate this issue and see if there is anything he could do to change or soften the problem. He also decides to take a proactive approach in future partnering activities. The next time he pairs students for an activity, he will explain why he is asking the students to work in pairs and describe appropriate ways to react when students hear the names of their partners.

When her first class begins that afternoon, Mrs. Lief doesn't remember exactly which girls were involved in the lunchroom situation. At the time it happened, she felt shocked and angry, but now it occurred to her that the group might have had a legitimate reason for moving. Maybe their table was getting too crowded, for instance, and they didn't want to make someone else find a new place.

As the students settle in their desks, she decides to scrap the lecture on respect that she had planned to fire off and begin English class instead with a sidebar on nonverbal communication. She introduces the term, then demonstrates a few examples and asks for their meaning: smiling versus frowning, giving someone an encouraging slap on the back versus sighing and looking up at the ceiling. Venturing further, she describes a couple of scenarios and asks how those actions could be read: one girl leans over and whispers to her friend when another person walks by, a group of guys in the cafeteria stand up and move to a different table just after someone sits down at their table. As Mrs. Lief mentions this last scenario, a couple of girls turn red and trade glances. Thankful that her lesson seems to have hit its mark, she ends the sidebar by encouraging the students to always think about the messages their actions convey. Perhaps they shouldn't whisper when others are around. If someone needs to move to a different table in the cafeteria, he should take the time to explain his reason to the person near him or invite her to come along.

Telling a Story

When a certain bratty or obnoxious behavior has infected a number of students at the same time, a well-told story may stop the epidemic. The power in stories for leading others to heart-felt change has been known since antiquity. The Old Testament prophet Nathan, for example, used a story to expose before King David the horror of his affair with Bathsheba and the scandalous murder of Uriah the Hittite.[3] In today's postmodern world, where young people are often more in tune to their feelings than to a sense of right and wrong, a story can be just as poignant.

A large treasury of folk tales exists for those who enjoy that genre. There are also true accounts of bullying with tragic endings that have worked well in situations where students single out and harass certain individuals. I like to share stories of my own life, when possible, because it's easier for me to paint a word picture of something I have experienced.

When told for corrective purposes, the intended lesson in a story is disguised so that troublesome students can be addressed without their guards raised. For this reason, it's best to reserve the story for a time when students would not be immediately suspicious of the teller's intentions. After the listeners are caught up in the feeling of the story, the point can be gently stated, if the students have not already figured it out.

I have an Old Faithful story for times when certain guys in a group need to rethink the way they relate to the opposite sex. Late in the winter, when the first whiffs of spring are in the air, some peculiar new emotions begin to stir at our sixth grade level. Considering the broad range in their outward physical development, it's mystifying how many internal male clocks strike "hormone time" all at once. Upon returning to school after a weekend away, a number of boys suddenly find girls to be extremely interesting creatures. Unfortunately for the males, the girls they are noticing are generally further along in their development and less attracted to the boys of their age. Somehow body functions and silliness aren't as appealing as sophistication and facial hair.

If one could merely sit back and watch, the interplay between pubescent males and females would be as amusing as any documentary on the Discovery Channel. However, when a person is trying to teach or motivate students with that sort of dynamic at work, the whole phenomenon is rather irksome. The story that follows is one I like to share when a bit of comic relief is needed. Though the humor of this incident is more easily conveyed through voice tone and facial expressions, the words themselves will have to suffice.

Early one April morning, I was in the basement of our home when I heard a strange racket in the furnace room. Cautiously I opened the door and peered into the darkness. Louder here, the noise was like a drum roll

---

3   In their book on using "emotional word pictures" to transform lives, Gary Smalley and John Trent refer to the prophet Nathan's story as one biblical example of this technique. Smalley, G. & Trent, J (1991). *The language of love.* Colorado Springs: Focus on the Family Publishing.

that would last for a couple of seconds then stop, only to start up again a few seconds later. The noise was actually inside the metal chimney pipe that comes out of our furnace. This pipe disappears inside a brick chimney where it extends all the way up to the peak of our roof. I decided to walk outside to see if anything was going on at the upper end of that pipe.

Do you know what was making the drum-roll sound? A woodpecker. He was sitting on top of our chimney, battering it with his beak. The sound was echoing down the long chimney pipe, all the way to the furnace room in the basement where I first heard it. I wondered how a bird could be so dumb as to look for tree bugs inside a metal pipe, so I did a little research after I got to school later that morning. It turns out that the woodpecker wasn't looking for food at all. Male woodpeckers will often knock their heads against metal objects to get the attention of females they want to impress.

Once the students have laughed a bit and cracked a few jokes about the story, it's time to share my own observations about the ways that guys their age sometimes act around girls. The trick here is to keep the girls from using the "lesson" as ammunition; they do not need to humiliate the boys further. For this reason it's best to keep the discussion general or to share examples which do not involve members of the class. In my case, a brief personal story is effective. As a sixth grader, I once caused a girl to cry. While we were riding on the school bus, I began to tease her, and she broke down in tears. The girl's reaction bewildered and embarrassed me. I actually had a crush on her and was only trying to get her attention! While this story attempts to remind the guys that girls are real persons with real feelings, there is a message in it for the girls as well: a male's outward behavior is not always the best indicator of who that person really is.

While stories are a favorite tool of mine, other art forms are helpful as well. A teacher can use a poem or a song, a painting, or even a simple drawing to get dialogue going, then skillfully connect it to a problem that needs to be addressed. Art, in its different forms, is a softening agent that opens hearts and minds to both problems and possibilities. Whereas a direct confrontation can sometimes encourage others to put up walls, a work of art can provide the diversion for students to get past themselves just long enough to see a situation from a new perspective.

Making Peace Through Dialogue

Because a heart-centered classroom climate encourages collaboration, it might seem curious that we began with three teacher-driven strategies for responding to conflict. In tweaking, straight talk, and story-telling, the teacher does not get on a soapbox, however. Our goal is to provide those making trouble an opportunity to change without singling them out, and to spare victims from embarrassment. Further, in situations not weighty enough for a meeting, a teacher-driven response seems a better use of time.

However, we also cannot neglect the importance of helping students resolve their issues through dialogue. When students clash with each other, dialogue is often the best remedy for several reasons. First, one quality you'll find in those marked by the name of Christ is not the *avoidance* of disagreement but a respectful way of *working through* disagreement. Conflict is an unfortunate yet expected part of living in a sinful world. Believers who encounter conflict look for ways to bring restoration, rather than seeking an eye for eye and a tooth for a tooth. In disagreement, they care as much for the needs and feelings of the other as they care for themselves. And in the search for common ground, they also grow in wisdom. A second reason for dialogue arises from our earlier discussion that respect is more than a behavior expectation: genuine respect grows out of the way we see each other. It's hard to imagine where anyone could find a more accurate "view" of another person's thoughts and emotions than through face-to-face communication. Finally, because it helps to build community, dialogue is a better choice than simply creating more rules and tougher consequences.

Despite the benefits of dialogue, some may question its effectiveness in situations that involve bullying. Because bullying has more to do with power and intimidation than with conflicting points of view, a peaceful, sincere conversation is not always feasible: a person who harasses others could use the dialogue as another opportunity to further belittle the victim. A teacher may initially need to confront the instigator one-to-one in order to protect the physical or emotional safety of those who are targets. Even so, teachers should consider an adult-mediated dialogue at some point in the process. As students grow older and more adept at keeping their vices under the radar, a teacher's warnings and threats lose potency. The most reliable weapon against harassment, in my experience, is open dialogue in the context of a classroom climate that values individual uniqueness over conformity.

Generally speaking, a dialogue between students in conflict can follow two different courses. Whereas the person who mediates cannot control what people say to each other, that person does foster attitudes that influence the direction of the talk. A teacher who sets out to determine "who started it" so that the appropriate consequence may be applied assumes a punitive stance. The punitive teacher encourages that troublesome attitude of defensiveness, which leads to denial and resentment. On the other hand, the mediator who assumes a redemptive—or restorative—approach fosters an attitude of honesty and forgiveness instead. That person realizes that people are complex creatures and that their problems are often complicated as well. The redemptive approach also understands that people tend to operate according to their perceptions and that, unless the perceptions are dealt with, a mere consequence will not permanently end a conflict.

Start and Steer

How does a go-between foster the attitudes we look for when seeking a resolution to conflict? Whether the meeting is a three-minute parley outside on the playground or a 30-minute conference involving an entire section of students, a few ground rules help to get the ship headed in the right direction.

Instead of asking a question in the form of "Who started this?," a teacher should begin the discussion with a different question, such as "What has happened here?" Obviously, that question will yield more honesty if it is voiced in a calm and non-threatening tone. Second, the conference will go nowhere if students interrupt each other, which is typically what happens when emotions are heated. Before individuals begin to share their respective sides of the story, the teacher would briefly spell out the rules of the meeting. Anyone who wishes to speak must wait their turn, for example. Also, those who respond should report specific actions rather than share personal impressions or call each other names.

A session involving only a few students can be modeled loosely in the style of a debate: one side shares the incident from its perspective, then the other is offered a turn to share. After the second side has spoken, each has an opportunity to respond to the comments of the other. A session involving a larger group requires a bit more structure. Seating the students in a circle generally works best. One fairly straightforward procedure is to explain that each person around the circle will be given two opportunities to speak. During his turn, a student may share his perspective of the story or respond to something that another person has said. Those who prefer not to speak may pass up their turn. After the opportunity to speak has completed two revolutions around the circle, the teacher may make some final observations or comments or invite the students to talk about where to go from here. Throughout the process, the teacher avoids taking sides, speaking only to clarify what someone has said or asking students to clarify their own statements. The decision on when and how to end is left to the teacher's discretion, of course. I prefer limiting whole-class discussions to two turns each, simply because some students enjoy prolonging a meeting in order to "waste" class time.

Even with the ground rules clearly stated, upset persons will typically interrupt each other or relay their impressions rather than the specific actions that have caused the trouble. For this reason, the teacher who mediates must be ready to cut off the interrupter and assure that person that she will get her turn. The mediator will also likely need to remind students that it doesn't do any good to say that someone "is being annoying" or that he is "acting like a jerk." Persons can change only when they know what behaviors are perceived as hurtful or annoying.

Finish and Follow Up

If the dialogue accomplishes what it is meant to, those who caused the trouble may feel enough gentle pressure from their peers to admit fault and commit to change their behavior or to restore what was broken. If not, the conversation will often yield information about who the instigators are, allowing the teacher to follow up later with one-to-one confrontations.

On the other hand, dialogue can also change the perceptions of victims. Sometimes those who felt hurt or angered by the actions of others will realize that their impressions were off regarding the other party's motivations. Either way, those who participate in a meeting with peers usually gain more insight than they would from an angry lecture by a frustrated teacher. Some of the benefits include a deeper awareness of the feelings of others and a better understanding of the way that one's own actions affect other people. Apologies are more sincere, and forgiveness is offered more willingly. Outcomes like these obviously represent an ideal, yet the ideal is more common than what one might expect, especially when the mediator assumes a restorative stance instead of a punitive stance.

Unfortunately, a single dialogue does not always resolve a conflict, especially in the event of unkindness or hostility. Those at fault may refuse to admit their wrongdoing or make light of the damage their actions have caused. Those hurt may harbor feelings of victimization or revenge. A meeting that flops should not be considered a failure. People and attitudes change slowly; heart-centered teachers continue to press forward and look for alternative paths. Thankfully, problems that remain unresolved after an initial attempt sometimes work themselves out over time as students realize the teacher cares enough to pay attention and to get involved.

Recently I became aware of two past cases of bullying in our school. The outcome looked bleak after the initial confrontation. One of the culprits had been strong-arming a student with minor special needs; in the other case, a boy had launched a cyber-bullying attack on a classmate. Yet more than two years later, each offender came to the side of his victim and defended that person in another bullying incident. In each situation, seeds were planted that, by God's grace, later bore fruit.

Caring for Bullies and Victims

As I mentioned earlier, the problem of bullying may require one-to-one intervention. Whereas some young people seem to derive a sick sense of pleasure from tormenting their peers, a closer look often reveals an underlying problem that needs to be addressed. Some bullies act out of a desire for power, others out of their insecurity. Developmentally, some children are not able to comprehend the feelings of the people around them. Still others struggle with social disorders, such as Asperger Syndrome, which impede their ability to understand social cues or to act appropriately in social situations.

Besides responding to the behavior itself, recall that heart-centered discipline attempts to address the root cause. Taking time to build relationships is a logical place to begin. For children who bully out of insecurity or a need for attention, a trusting relationship with an adult may prove the best remedy. If connecting with the person does not alleviate the problem, a teacher may still uncover clues about the cause.

Bullies who cannot empathize with the feelings of others may need an approach that seems more behavioristic, an approach that includes consequences. Is this type of response at odds with a heart-centered approach to discipline? In the context of love, no. As we saw in Chapter Seven, teachers who care enough to rescue a wayward student from the destructive path they are on show grace, even when they have to get tough. In doing so, teachers not only seek to restore the safety of victims; they want to turn bullies themselves from a road that leads inevitably to loneliness and trouble. Any behavior plan that a teacher sets up for a student (or *with* a student) would also include ways to reinforce acts of kindness. Keeping in mind the bigger goals of heart-centered discipline, teachers do not neglect the periodic opportunity to talk with bullies about the effects of their behavior, about what is inappropriate as well as appropriate.

When necessary, heart-centered teachers also help sensitive students to reinterpret the behavior of their peers. Children and young people have convoluted ways of expressing endearment for one another, and thin-skinned students easily feel victimized by the jokes and pranks of their peers. Attentive teachers rightly encourage jokesters and wisecrackers to be conscious of the feelings of others. Yet a caring teacher also shows concern for the emotional health of students who feel victimized. A dose of one-on-one teaching is often useful in helping sensitive students learn to enjoy the banter of their peers rather than reacting to it.

Remaining Vigilant

Even though most teachers would prefer that their students report harassment, victims often choose to stay quiet for fear of what their tormentors will do if an adult intervenes. Their predicament is understandable, of course. Yet any sort of bullying—public or private—is still intolerable in a heart-centered classroom. What can teachers do about harassment that occurs under the radar?

I have experienced a reasonable degree of success by regularly reminding students that everyone has a right to feel safe at our school. Whereas I do not condone "tattling" (reporting misbehavior for the sole purpose of getting someone in trouble), students need to tell an adult if someone is getting hurt. That reminder conveys to both victims and potential bullies alike that protecting children from bullying is a priority for me.

Second, if a victim of harassment asks me not to confront the offender, I assure the person that I will avoid any sort of intervention that arouses suspicions of tattling. The next step is alerting other teachers to the problem so that together we increase our surveillance in places where the bullying has occurred or may occur. In this way, we have been able to catch offenders in the act and immediately confront them. Even the strategy of responding with a more visible presence curbs much of the unkindness that is reported to us.

Conclusion

By now we have examined several strategies for addressing conflict among students. Heart-centered teachers maintain a constant vigil for small problems that could signal or lead to bigger problems. When conflicts do arise, they take care to determine the nature of the problem and consider how their response will affect the classroom community. In some cases, a one-way talk is the best plan to minimize hurt and helping wrongdoers to see a situation from a new perspective. In other cases, dialogue is the most appropriate way to restore victims and offenders.

Whereas any one of these strategies may help to remedy an isolated incident, the problem of a malicious dynamic within a class cannot be resolved through a single intervention. Uprooting unkindness begins with the cultivation of an atmosphere where students are encouraged to respect each other and to cooperate, as we saw in Chapter Five. Spiteful behavior is also reduced in a climate where divergent thinking is welcome and where students are encouraged to tactfully challenge the thinking of one another, as we saw in Chapter Six.

When conflict does arise, teachers who are committed to changing a negative dynamic among students care enough to get involved. With fortitude they press ahead on all fronts, working with individuals, small groups, or entire sections of students when necessary. In disciplinary action, they look beyond retribution to restoration and healing. Let's take a look now at resolving conflict between students and teachers.

CHAPTER 12:
TAMING THE ELEPHANT

Beyond Control

Unable to focus, comical Royce diverted attention away from his learning challenges by imitating people or contorting his face into quirky expressions. I had to admit that the guy was funny—he could crack up a stone with his antics. How do you get math or history to compete with a live sideshow?

Peyton, the other humorist, was more of a thorn. Unlike most of his classmates who struggled in school, Peyton needed to devote only a small portion of his mental capacity to learning. The remainder of his attention could be used in comic relief. To add to my woes, Peyton's style was to work undercover; students laughed at him only when my back was turned. I suspect that I was the butt of most of his silent comedy.

Unfortunate Philip never really caused trouble; he just attracted it. Operating at a deficit of social skills, he was a bunny garbed in neon during open season. Anyone who wanted to advance his own status by shooting somebody else down had an easy target with Philip. I was always jumping in to pull him out of the range of fire or to patch up his latest wounds.

In addition to the frequent snickers and gibes, a foul-smelling cloud of resistance had filtered in from somewhere. Complaining was on the rise. Students griped about assignments and balked at any activity that didn't seem like fun. Positive participation, meanwhile, had bottomed out. Whereas kids were motivated to debate homework assignments, few could muster the energy to discuss ideas or to ask questions.

Despite the difficulties, rowdy classes were nothing new to me. With nearly twenty past years of classroom experience I had seen my share of challenges. A steady dose of meaningful teaching and consistent consequences were usually enough to get students on track, sooner or later. The perplexity about this bunch was that after three months I still wasn't making headway. If anything, I was losing ground.

Eventually the mystery began to unravel. Sharon, and Bonnie, and Ron weren't bad kids; they just didn't care for me. Because they rarely got into trouble, I was slow to notice their effect on the group as a whole. It seemed that the three had been gifted with some pretty exceptional leadership skills. When they giggled at Royce or Peyton, others guffawed. If one of them sneered at Philip, somebody else was sure to make a comment. I even noticed complainers checking with them for approval after lobbing protest-missiles in my direction.

It was clear that the collective attitude of the three had propagated and spread itself through the room. Because I now felt at odds with the entire group, every misdeed took the appearance of personal affront. Some of the behavior *was* mean-spirited, of course, but I was too consumed with fighting it to rise above and redirect it.

Conflict between students and teachers is burdensome because of a number of concerns that matter a great deal, at least to the teacher. Take the ego, for instance: "I'm the teacher and my students aren't listening to me!" A person's self-confidence can take a hit, too: "I really stink at this job." Or, a teacher may worry about his or her reputation: "What will people think if I can't control these kids?"

The idiom "elephant in the room" refers to a truth that is obvious to everyone and yet difficult to address. Even though rampant negativity is easy to see, keeping it in check is a complex undertaking—almost like restraining an elephant. Elephants in classrooms are intimidating. Teachers who lack the skills or the nerve to address a negative dynamic sometimes choose to ignore the problem, hoping it will grow weary and wander off. Turning a blind eye to mischief, though, usually just encourages it to become more bold. When ignored, the proverbial elephant saunters to the middle of the room, shoves a few desks aside, and makes itself comfy.

On the other hand, some teachers try to overpower negative dynamics. To them the issue is not actually *conflict*, which suggests an equality between parties, a situation in which the adult and the students need to come together and work out their differences. These teachers label the problem as "insubordination" or "unruliness"—teachers don't have *conflicts* with students. People who assume this stance usually take the route that I cautioned against in Chapter Eleven, merely ramping up the intensity of their classroom management plan. However, because a classroom dynamic resides more in a collective attitude than in a certain behavior, it seldom yields to stricter rules and heavier consequences alone. Negative dynamics feed on anger and ultimatums. As the teacher becomes ever more reactive, the elephant climbs up and perches itself happily on the podium where it can soak up all of the negative attention it craves.

Heart-centered teachers use a different option. Instead of ignoring the brute or fighting it, they seek to tame it. Taming an attitude requires that teachers first build the trust of their students, something we have discussed at length already. They also respond in ways that will calm the students down instead of revving them up. Finally, they consistently demonstrate their commitment to build a collaborative atmosphere where people and ideas are respected and where learning is central.

Retraining the Eyes

Once again, the first hurdle is to readjust our own focus. Though it's easy to characterize a group by a few predominant behaviors, lumping all of the students into one category is often self-defeating. Teachers who believe that their struggles lie with an entire class become reactive and spiteful, or get to feeling gloomy and rejected. In addition, viewing the group as a horde disregards the persons within that group who do not share the sentiment of defiance.

Another part of this readjustment is the paradigm shift we talked about earlier: learning to view behavior problems as learning problems. If we accept that students act largely according to their perceptions, then a classroom dynamic becomes an opportunity for teaching rather than an occasion for combat. The goal shifts away from finding the right maneuver to straighten everyone out, to helping the students see and act differently. Teaching here does not denote sermonizing; it means availing oneself of all of the tools available in ordinary teaching. Let's look at some ways to deal with teacher-versus-student dynamics, in the spirit of heart-centered discipline.

Clowns and Ringleaders

The reputation or character of a class is often influenced by a "character" within the class. Clowns siphon attention away from learning through entertainment, while ringleaders instigate negative behavior but seldom step into the limelight. We'll deal with the classroom comic first.

On the positive side, humor can serve the purpose of learning. If it causes us to look at something in a new way, our minds retain the concept longer. Obviously, laughter also makes learning more enjoyable. Talking with a comedian, then, about the appropriateness or the timing of one's comments would redirect that student more than merely criticizing. A heart-centered teacher might show the student that humor works best when it's not overdone, when it contributes to the topic rather than steals from the show. If a person will not or cannot control his antics, a teacher will need to limit the student's potential for gaining attention, perhaps by moving him to a less conspicuous place. The goal in that response is not to punish but to provide training in what is appropriate. Follow-up conversations should affirm the gift of humor while pointing out the effect of comedy that is misguided or overdone.

Removing a clown from center-stage can introduce a "rebound dynamic" when the others in the class feel that you've stolen their fun. Not long ago, this happened when I resorted to sending a hyperactive comedian to the Resource Room for half a day. Two girls with a significant amount of power in the group organized a grade-wide protest arguing for his "release." Eventually I was able to talk the students through the issue by complimenting them on their concern for their classmate and by explaining that the separation, though painful for all of us, was our way of helping the person "learn" how to learn in the regular classroom. They could also help their friend to stay in the classroom by not laughing at his pranks and by gently reminding him to listen.

Sometimes it also helps to remind students about the purpose of classroom time and the purpose of breaks. "Class, I know that it would be fun to just laugh and joke around with each other, but that is what break times are for. The time in our classroom is for learning; we need to use it well." Ultimately, the context of a collaborative atmosphere usually minimizes the problem. As students grow more connected to their learning and become involved in the learning process, their need for outside amusement diminishes. When a teacher remains unswervingly committed to meaningful instruction, students may eventually grow tired of the antics of class jokers. Some will even begin to reprimand the person on their own, which is always a fortunate turn of events for the teacher!

On the other hand, sometimes a class is dominated by one or two members whose opinions apparently outweigh those of everyone else. When any ringleader in a group holds that kind of power, gaining their approval becomes an all-consuming enterprise for the others. At one person's whim, any learning activity, brand of clothing, extra-curricular activity, or cafeteria food is prized or rejected. A strong leader can also turn large numbers of students against their teacher or any fellow classmate.

A redirective personal confrontation with a ringleader would follow a similar vein of affirming the leadership gift while guiding the person to lead in more positive ways. Eventual consequences, should they be deemed necessary, would be followed up again with discussions about the goodness of the person's gift that has become distorted.

In addition, however, a teacher should not forego a sincere attempt to determine the nature of this misguided struggle for power. One commonality I have seen at different times boils down to a lack of trust in the teacher. The student feels bored in class or perceives inconsistent discipline. Turning others against the teacher is the easiest way to gain control. Hence the futility of overpowering a ringleader: punishing only turns the person into a martyr or hero. Must a teacher cater to the student then? Of course not.

Heart-centered teachers seek to base their decisions upon *what* is right rather than *who* is right. Whereas student input helps to inform a decision, input does not determine the decision. The teacher honors the student as an image bearer by listening to the person's ideas, but she also trains the student by demonstrating what sorts of ideas are worth sharing and insisting that ideas are shared in respectful ways.

If a teacher can gain the trust of a ringleader, a negative classroom dynamic will usually disperse. Unfortunately, the kingpins of a class are not always so willing to oblige, in which case the teacher still has to deal with the larger group. Teachers of younger students might try initiating a game of "Simon Says" and follow up with a discussion about how silly it looks when people allow others to make all of their decisions for them.

Teachers of older students can hold similar discussions that are appropriate to the ages of their children.

Any conversation about these matters will take root, though, only within the larger context of a heart-centered atmosphere. A classroom climate where different perspectives are welcomed, for example, is an environment that encourages students to make their own choices rather than take their cues from domineering classmates.

Complaints and Bellyaches

"Ms. Smith, why do you pick on the boys? The girls never get in trouble here."

"Well, Isaac, if the girls made as much noise as the boys did, they'd be facing the same consequences. It doesn't matter who is causing the problem; if someone disrupts class, he's in trouble."

"Yeah? Well Allie and Naomi whisper all the time. Why don't you ever do anything to them?"

"Isaac, that remark just cost you a detention."

"See, there she goes again."

"Christian, now you've got one, too."

"Same song, different verse."

"Tyler!"

Public whining or protesting is a classic spoiler of classroom climate, and teachers should become skillful at diverting it. While not every whiner in a classroom carries the same potency, a rabble-rouser with influence can draw teacher and students into a contention where no one wins. In heart-centered classrooms, however, where teachers actually encourage a certain degree of student input, what can be done about grumbling?

Prevention is probably the best cure for public complaining—it simply should not be allowed. Students are able to express their grievances to the teacher in private; they do not need an audience of classmates. A life lesson about disgruntlement applies here, regardless of context—classroom, workplace, or political arena. Public protest gains attention, but it seldom results in positive change. If anything, it fosters defensiveness or obstinacy by those with authority. Though this rule carries no guarantees, comments are more likely to obtain a listening ear if voiced respectfully and privately. In a heart-centered classroom, then, it makes sense to provide a procedure for expressing disgruntlement and train students to follow it.

As I said in an earlier chapter, some teachers make a suggestion box available. They follow up on the notes placed there by talking with the students who submit them. After listening carefully, they either provide an explanation for their actions or agree that something needs to change and commit to making that change. Of course there are other ways to make oneself available to students with grievances; the point is not in the method but in teaching young people that voicing concerns quietly is more effective than stirring up stink in class.

How should a teacher respond to a student who complains in class instead of utilizing a more respectful way? If a procedure is serious enough to be addressed in the rules of the classroom, an appropriate consequence ought to accompany a rule against public grumbling. Sometimes, however, a disgruntlement gains too much momentum among students to be diverted with a penalty, forcing the teacher to address the concern in class before learning can continue.

In this situation, teachers need to consider the nature of the complaint and their own rapport or influence with the group before choosing a response. Some complaints have no legitimacy because the teacher has made a reasonable decision and has already provided rationale. Persons can respond to "bellyaching" in a couple of ways. Experienced teachers who have enough confidence and the right rapport may choose to toss back a bit of humor. If a funny retort is done skillfully, the students will soon be smirking at how silly they sound. One teacher I know tells her students to applaud when they feel upset with her. The angrier they feel, the louder they may clap. Before long, everyone is laughing. In situations where teachers have not developed that level of trust among students, however, humor will often backfire and should be avoided. Sometimes a curt response is the best way to put out the fire. Unnecessary complaining has no place in a heart-centered classroom, and telling students so in plain and unmistakable terms is entirely appropriate.

On the other hand, some complaints toward a teacher do have validity, either because the teacher has made a mistake and needs to admit it, or because there is a misunderstanding that needs to be straightened out. The teacher who errs ought to apologize, if an apology is warranted, and then try to set things right again. Those who acknowledge their mistakes and who offer sincere apologies model an appropriate response to correction. Students cannot be expected to take responsibility for wrongdoing if they learn under teachers who become defensive in the face of criticism.

The teacher who has been misunderstood or misrepresented takes the complaint as an opportunity to explain himself. If the group seems upset with the teacher at the time an issue is raised, however, it is often best to acknowledge the feeling and commit to dealing with the matter later when both the teacher and the students are calm enough to see the situation more objectively. Unless an explanation is very clear and the teacher can remain unruffled in communicating it, the problem is likely to escalate into an argument that no one can win. Ms. Smith, the teacher at the beginning of this section, could have initially said, "Isaac, I see that you're frustrated with me. Come see me later and we'll talk about it." The wait would have provided Isaac time to cool down, and it would have afforded space for Ms. Smith to think about the wisest way to respond. At some point during this later discussion, the teacher would also address Isaac's inappropriate choice to challenge her on an issue during class.

More than likely, the timing of Isaac's complaint was an attempt to spark an argument in class, something any prudent teacher would want to avoid. If Isaac were to react against Ms. Smith's invitation to visit privately about the matter, she should briefly explain her reason for waiting and get the class back to their learning. "If we try to work through this now, when some of us are feeling upset, nobody is going to be happy with the result." Then, with a tone of finality, "We will talk about it later."

Sometimes a teacher-student conflict arises that cannot be pinned down to one certain behavior or incident. The students may have become resistant to learning, as we discussed in Chapter Six. Perhaps they ignore warnings and remain impervious to discipline. Or, for some reason, they've decided that they do not like the teacher, and though no one says this outright, their body language is unmistakable. The class meeting can become a turning point in difficult situations like these.

Lending an Ear Without Lending Control

Moderating a discussion about a conflict—when you are personally involved in that conflict—is no easy task. You will play two seemingly conflicting roles simultaneously—on the one hand modeling an appropriate way to work through a dispute, seeing someone else's point of view and perhaps even agreeing to compromise—while on the other hand preserving your authority and not allowing students to take advantage of you. Even more challenging is the reality that you'll feel inclined to take some of their comments personally; yet in order to remain in charge, you will have to appear unaffected.

A heart-centered class meeting cannot be allowed to degenerate into a mere gripe session; though negative feelings will be aired, the end result must be productive. One way to maintain an overall positive tone is to set clear parameters for the discussion. If the meeting was called to discuss problems related to the learning—difficulty of the material, relevance of the material, or a perceived lack of variety in the lessons, for instance—the teacher might begin by reviewing the goals for the learning unit, then proceed by asking the students if they feel the goals are being met. A second question would obviously follow: if certain goals are not being met, what are the students' ideas for meeting the goals more effectively? If, on the other hand, the problem stems from chronic misbehavior, such as incessant talking out of turn, the teacher could state the problem and ask students if they can vocalize why talking out of turn is a problem. A follow-up question might ask students for ideas on solving the problem.

If teachers feel that they are too connected to a problem in order to moderate a civil discussion about it, another way to respond is to have students write out their comments instead. I related one particular use of this strategy in Chapter Six. The teacher opens the meeting by talking briefly about the problem, then invites the students to write about the issue from their perspective. Later the teacher reads the comments outside of class, taking time to consider the best course of action. A wise person would show that the writing was taken seriously by summarizing the students' concerns, by incorporating some of the ideas expressed, or by at least thanking the students for helping the teacher to know more about the problem. Though not every idea voiced through the activity can be carried out, sometimes merely providing an opportunity for young people to air their feelings is the best neutralizer when a classroom atmosphere has gone sour.

Diverting Defiance

Whereas students sometimes antagonize by complaining, they can also set their teachers up for a clash by ignoring the boundaries. Not all misbehavior falls into this category, obviously. The forgetful child might not intend to leave that pencil in her locker, and the hyperactive one does not always purposely blurt things out. The type of misbehavior we're looking at is not of the blunder variety. It is a maneuver, and the intention is to challenge or defy the teacher.

Even though the attitude that steers this sort of behavior may be unmistakable, fixating on it leads a teacher to become vindictive or downhearted. Harping about the disposition of a group also feeds the negativity. While it can't be denied that an "elephant" has wandered into the room, teachers may wish to discipline themselves to appear oblivious to it, responding only to the behavior and not to what they think the behavior means. Let's look at another situation.

After Mrs. Van Dyk gets her computer connected to the projector, she notices a couple of students nibbling on snacks, despite her reminders this week that eating is for break time. Fed up with their disobedience, she decides it's time to create a consequence for eating in class: from now on, any food that appears in this room will be confiscated. A couple of days later, as she finishes writing a sentence on the board, Mrs. Van Dyk hears the rattle of paper and turns to see Karen shove something into her pocket. She and the two other girls in her pod, Barb and Beth, attempt an innocent grin, but they are not very convincing with their lips tightly closed. In the next group, Jander's hand shifts to hide something under his desk. His partner Randy avoids eye contact. The side of his face has a bulge in it and he seems to be trying hard not to swallow.

The students knew where the line had been drawn, and they had stepped over it. Defiance. Mrs. Van Dyk feels angry; these kids deserve a good chewing out. Yet preferring to avoid a showdown in class, she chooses to simply carry out the consequence of the rule and not draw attention to the recalcitrance in the air. Without a break in her teaching, she picks up the waste bin and holds it in front of the three girls until each has spit out her candy. Then she heads over to Jander and waits for him to deposit the brownie he had been sharing with Randy. More paper rustling now.

Mrs. Van Dyk turns her head to John, who looks directly back at her, then empties the crumbs from a bag of chips into his mouth and drops it on the floor. The teacher, keeping her cool, again diverts a face-off in class. After thinking for a second, she holds the trash bin out for John. "Looks like you missed the can. Would you throw that bag in there for me, please?" Temporarily derailed by the teacher's calmness, John looks blankly back at her, then reaches down and throws the paper in the bin. "Stop by my desk before you leave the room today, please."

Mrs. Van Dyk resumes the lesson, allowing herself the rest of class time to let her anger subside and plan the conversation with John. Obviously he will need to serve a consequence for his defiance. Without following through, no one will take her seriously anymore. Yet something really must be bugging him to cause him to act this way. In the end, she decides to spend the bulk of the confrontation finding out why he behaved so belligerently. Then she will give him a consequence that she believes is appropriate.

When a teacher can eventually manage a positive change in a group's behavior, she may notice a shift in attitude as well. Since it's not realistic to transform everyone's conduct in a single sweep when multiple misbehaviors are present, she would focus on the most troubling actions first, then gradually work through the others.

A Context for Consequences

Sometimes it becomes necessary to impose a consequence on an entire group of students instead of an individual. The discussion about imposing class-wide consequences assumes that the teacher has already made sincere attempts at a collaborative atmosphere. As mentioned earlier, students treated as passive recipients of learning are more likely to seek control in harmful ways. We will also presume that the teacher tries to confront individuals in private, wherever possible. When a person does need to impose a consequence on the group, a heart-centered approach follows two guidelines.

First, the consequence fits the nature of the offense. A group who misuses a privilege loses that privilege for awhile. A lesson hindered by disruptions may need to be completed during a time when the students would have preferred another activity. A teacher whose trust was broken may temporarily have to adjust her teaching style, instructing in ways that allow for closer teacher surveillance, though naturally less student freedom.

Is it fair that a minority of cooperative students in a group should "suffer" under a class-wide consequence? Unfortunately, when many are involved in wrongdoing, determining who needs the discipline and who doesn't becomes guesswork. Further, attempting to single out the few students "above reproach" runs the risk of alienating those persons from the rest of the class. The only way around this problem is to remember that retribution is not the end goal in redemptive discipline. Our target is to create a classroom climate where learning is meaningful and enjoyable. When class consequences are imposed in this context, the need for them usually self-eliminates, and students who want to learn are eventually more free to do so. To answer the question about fairness, then, we have to think of it relatively. Subjecting a few innocent students to a group consequence isn't exactly fair. However, if the consequence removes an obstruction to learning and ultimately leads to a more positive atmosphere, in the long run the change provides more justice to those students than ignoring a problem that bogs down the learning.

Second, in confronting a group, heart-centered teachers retain their authority by redirecting instead of reacting. Anger can be a great attention getter. Yet teachers who do not follow an outburst by collecting themselves and pointing the group in a new direction play directly into the students' antagonism. A person operating out of a teaching model—one that turns behavior problems into teaching and learning opportunities—would soon begin to reflect on ways to lead the students forward.

Let's consider the teacher model for discipline in the light of classroom dynamics. When a group struggles with learning a new concept, effective teachers ask questions to determine where the problem lies. They may try different explanations, share an illustration or story, or assign extra practice. Effective teachers are careful not to leave the impression that the group is too dense to learn; instead they look for progress and offer encouragement. A heart-centered teacher leading a class out of a negative dynamic would attempt to operate according to that same pattern. If they address an attitude or behavior pattern, they listen as much as they talk. As the days and weeks go by, they find different ways to show connections between behavior and its effects. They might require the group to practice procedures that have become problem areas. Finally, heart-centered teachers encourage, despite the obstinate vibes students send their way. Their role is to lead; not to react.

Light-hearted consequences created for offenses that are less serious can also help to diffuse a negative dynamic. One year several students came to my class with the habit of tipping back on their chairs. Despite my rule about chair tipping and its rationale, they continued the habit. Finally I wrote out five different penalties for chair tipping on a poster. Then I placed five slips of paper in a jar, each with a letter that corresponded to one of the consequences on the poster. From that point, anybody who tipped her chair had to reach into the jar and serve the consequence indicated on the paper she chose. Whereas the penalty itself might have seemed unpleasant, the suspense of selecting one's own consequence was somewhat diverting.[1]

My penalty for complaining in class was born out of a similar problem. A dozen years ago, some students noticed that public complaining was a "hot button" in my temperament and began to use it to their advantage. Eventually I created a consequence that would reinforce an appropriate way of venting and potentially change their mood as well. The complaint penalty involves a couple of steps. During the next break, they have to write out their grievance on a slip of paper, then "practice"

---

1   For your information, the consequences were as follows: (a) Copy a list of four reasons for the chair rule on a paper during lunch break. (b) Stack chairs for the rest of the class at the end of the day. (c) Lose your chair and kneel at your desk for the next thirty minutes of class. (d) During lunch break, copy a picture of a stick person sitting at a desk with appropriate posture. (e) Reminder: apologize to the teacher and thank him for the reminder.

inserting it in the suggestion box. They walk from their desk to deposit the paper and then retrieve it to repeat the process several times. When they are finished, we discuss the complaint together. Because most students are laughing at themselves by this time, reaching an understanding on the problem is usually not difficult.

Conclusion

A group dynamic is essentially a controlling force within a group. The bottom line in addressing a negative dynamic is this question: will the dynamic also control the teacher? Those teachers who remain unaffected (at least visibly) by a group's disposition stand the best chance of heading their dynamic in a different direction.

We have surveyed a number of strategies for redirecting classroom dynamics. Yet no strategy by itself, or even a collection of strategies, has the potency to shift a collective attitude. The key resides in an entire classroom climate that we labor to create, an atmosphere built up through trusting relationships, a collaborative atmosphere, a redirective approach to discipline, and a patient, persevering outlook that trusts in God's timing.

In case you were wondering, my year with the difficult class ended well. No, the behavior problems did not completely disappear. The obstacles of personality combinations and behavior conditions are sometimes too difficult to overcome. However, misbehavior was eventually reduced to a tolerable level.

The change for which I was most grateful was the shift in attitude among the ringleaders and its subsequent improvement in the temperament of the class. Of course I don't imagine that my name would appear on their list of favorite teachers; our personalities were just too different for me to attain that level of respect. Though I like it when students appreciate me, I had to remind myself that their affections aren't a requirement for heart-centered teaching. The more valuable quality that I did gain was their trust. As I made time and space for their ideas and slowly redirected their misguided notions about the nature of learning, they began to display a more cooperative spirit. Ron became a positive leader in group projects. Sharon grew tired of the clowning behavior and started telling some of her classmates to grow up. Whereas Bonnie was more reluctant to come around, the two of us did share a couple of laughs in the final weeks of school, and once I saw her reach out to help Philip in a disheartening moment. Any sign of growth, no matter how small, is an occasion for thanksgiving! Praise God.

CHAPTER 13:
HOPE AND A FUTURE

Un-extreme Makeovers

You could still see the house up on the hill, about a kilometer from the road. A few buildings and half a dozen trees had been spared, to keep it company. The old barn was gone and the mulberry grove was gone, and the wooden bridge over the creek in the lane had been replaced with a large culvert. When I was young, an occasional spring flood would loosen the planks on that bridge and carry them off downstream. One of those floods came when my mother was about to give birth to my sister. With steady labor contractions, my mom had to balance her way over one of the spare planks, above the rushing current, to the other side where she could catch a ride to the hospital in a neighbor's pickup.

Now, thirty years later my parents and a bunch of relatives were back to fix up the house for my uncle and aunt, who wanted to live closer to my aging grandma. They had known that the latest tenants were not obsessive about neatness, yet it was shocking to see how badly the place had degenerated under the renters' neglect.

The yard was a landfill of pizza boxes, junked cars, and dog kennel parts. Though the ground outside was soggy from a recent shower, there was no need to remove one's shoes inside the door; the living room carpet was about as clean as the bare spot in front where the fellow had parked his truck. His family and the hunting dogs who cohabitated with them had relocated to another state, but a horde of rodents were still squatting on the property. Before they moved, my dad had inquired about a pistol he saw lying on the bookshelf. "Oh that," said the tenant, "I use it to shoot the rats when they run through here."

Houses in need of rehabilitation are typically the most resistant to change, and this one was no exception with holes in the roof to be patched, electric wires to be rerun, and plumbing to be replaced. Even a couple of the basement walls, bowed in from water pressure in the soil, had to be pushed back out and straightened. The clean-up work seemed just as endless. Folks worked for days, scrubbing and mopping, trimming back weeds and hauling trash away.

Having literally gone to the dogs for so long, the property would never resume the original charm that anyone remembered, yet sometimes the character of a place is found in the memories made there, in the relationships formed or renewed. The work, unpleasant as it was, reunited siblings and cousins who had grown apart over the years. Anyone who showed up, even out of curiosity, was handed a hammer, a weed whacker, or a scoop shovel. Aside from an occasional argument about whether a particular outbuilding needed paint or a bulldozer, there was also plenty of laughter. A circle of lawn chairs appeared under the old Chinese elm, and coffee again became a time of day, instead of just a drink. At one point my dad surprised everyone when he tinkered one of the abandoned cars to life and drove it across the yard. It was his turn to be surprised, though, when the brake pedal went to the floor without catching. Unable to stop, he crashed the car through the side of the corncrib.

Perhaps you've heard of Ty Pennington, the charming carpenter-model, who took home renovation to the extreme for nearly a decade on ABC's reality television series, *Extreme Makeover: Home Edition*. On a typical show, Pennington would send a needy family on a fantasy vacation to Disney, then mobilize his crew and half the town to transform their shack into a dream home in seven days. One reviewer described Ty, who grew up as a carpenter and later performed miracles on people's homes, a "modern-day messiah."

Though you couldn't help but admire a generous guy like Ty, he is only a dim reflection of Master Carpenter, who hangs around a lot longer than Pennington ever did and often works at a pace that is miraculously slow. Instead of moving *on* to the worksite, he moves *in*, while the place is still a complete mess. On a timescale somewhat proportional to our obstinacy, he goes to work on our brokenness.

Sometimes the people around us are his tools. It's never pleasant to hear that our lives are askew, yet looking back we've all experienced the Master's touch through the admonishment of others. Other times he allows us to face the natural consequences of our actions. Or, in allowing us to grow older, he installs a new set of eyes, windows that help us to see what we were blind to in our younger years. Of course some people's lives are transformed almost instantly, and through the testimonies of those women and men we see that Christ really can do anything. Yet most often, about the only part of the restoration process that could be called "extreme" is God's own patience.

Near the beginning of this book you saw the basic presumptions of a heart-centered approach to classroom management. Now that we have explored teaching and discipline in the light of this concept, we return to a few of the themes in Scripture. My purpose here is not so much to "prove" a biblical basis for heart-centered discipline as it is to pass along some of the encouragement I have found there as I try to practice heart-centered discipline.

Perfect, Yet Not Always Consistent

Through the storytellers of the Old Testament, we come to know a God who is not like an insentient traffic camera that issues penalties with machine-like uniformity and indifference. Instead we see a living personal Being, whose emotions about wrongdoing range from sadness and disappointment to anger and regret. Sometimes he chooses to ignore transgression; other times he bestows lavish grace. With righteous indignation he justly serves his people what they've got coming, or he allows himself to be talked out of the consequences they have earned. Finally, despite an unfavorable history, God is not inclined to give up on people—at least not as quickly as we usually are.

I think of the narrative of the Judges, a classic illustration of obstinate human nature and the heart of a God who loves the people he must reprove. Repeatedly the Israelites find themselves in trouble because they've chased after false gods. After enduring some oppression from their enemies, they typically regret their error and cry out to be saved. God's willingness to rescue the Israelites from punishment, despite a cycle of behavior that recurs over and over, both amazes and mystifies me.

One of my favorite examples is his response to the people of Israel in Chapter 10, where they ask for deliverance from the Philistines and the Ammonites after still another love affair with idols. At first it looks as if the people have finally reached the breaking point of God's mercy. "Go and cry out to the gods you have chosen," God retorts with a hint of sarcasm. "Let them save you when you are in trouble." Unswayed in their groveling, however, the Israelites confess that they have sinned. "Do with us whatever you think best, but please rescue us now." They discard their foreign gods and serve the Lord. Then the narrator reports that God "could bear Israel's misery no longer."

To me, those are some of the most profound words in scripture. The track record of the Israelites does not indicate that their loyalty will last, and indeed we find in subsequent episodes that it doesn't. Still, God relieves them of the penalty they are justly paying and offers yet another chance.

Are there parallels between the work of God in Scripture and the work he calls us to carry on in our classrooms? In some respects, no. Unlike God, we are stuck in sin. At the end of the day, we still have to admit that we've made mistakes, that some of our misery is a result of things we have fouled up all by ourselves. Also, in coping with uncooperative students we may not retaliate, as vengeance is reserved for God alone.

Created in God's image, though, we all reflect certain aspects of his character. Occasional disappointment and anger, for example, are emotions that even God seems to experience in working with people. It must be okay, then, to feel lousy about the way our kids behave; becoming angry occasionally is a natural response to wrongdoing.

However, it is also permissible to let love be our guide rather than the "system." Thank God we're not mere traffic cameras. We're allowed to look beneath the behavior before choosing a response. Sometimes adhering to the discipline plan is the most loving way to keep an individual or group on track; in proper perspective, even a painful consequence is an act of mercy, as we saw in Chapter Seven. In other cases, a gentle confrontation, in lieu of the standard consequence, furnishes a more convincing nudge and opens the door for God to work in a person's heart.

Furthermore, we're allowed to hope for what we cannot see. Whether mercy is provided through the consequence or in place of it, we can trust in what God is doing with the person over the long term. Whereas repeated misbehavior may call for stiffer penalties or tighter boundaries, resistance must not be allowed to squelch the relationship with the person. Part of forgiving is trusting that the individual is ultimately in God's hands. By trusting God, we are free to love.

How do we know that the grace we extend will not be abused, that the student will not backslide and disappoint us again? We can't be certain really, and in this unknown lies the potential for both pain and pleasant surprise in heart-centered discipline. God "foreknew" that people would soon forget his goodness, yet he bestowed grace anyway. Walking by faith, I can follow his lead.

A Good Friend of Mine

Teachers who despair over negative attitudes may find a kindred spirit in the poet Jeremiah. Along with other people like Zephaniah, Habakkuk, and Obadiah, Jeremiah shared the rather thankless task of identifying the wrong in people's lives and warning them of impending judgment. The thing that sets him apart, though, is his frequent despondency. Despite the bold rebukes he fires off to his countrymen and their false prophets, Jeremiah intermittently lays bare the deep struggles of his soul. At one point he even curses the day he was born.

Personally, I have never been the target of a murder plot, and I've never served time in a muddy cistern. No chief executive has ever cut my writing apart and thrown it in a fire. On the other hand, I can relate to wanting what's best for someone and having them hate me for it. I've been bad-mouthed by students who thought I was out to get them when my intentions were for them to succeed at school and to enjoy their learning. From my perspective, the connection between the behavior of certain young people and their misery seems so obvious. If they would just change their outlook, stop resisting authority and love the good—or at least give the good a chance—would they not find their teachers more agreeable, or even fun?

One often-quoted verse from Jeremiah's writings appears in a personal letter to the people of his homeland. "'For I know the plans I have for you,' declares the LORD, 'plans to prosper you and not to harm you, plans to give you hope and a future.'" It's a passage that has become especially popular at graduation ceremonies. The first people to hear these words, however, were not commemorating any great achievements. On the contrary, they were paying the consequences of their wrong. Despite repeated warnings from Jeremiah and other prophets of the Lord, the Jews had continued to walk a path that led away from a loving and trusting relationship with God. Now they were under exile in Babylon, the very sort of punishment that had been spelled out by Moses some 800 years before.

It's interesting that the "weeping prophet" would write a letter of encouragement to people who had ignored and even persecuted him, who were now receiving the just reward of unfaithfulness to their King. Similar to Jeremiah, heart-centered teachers are bound to get down in the dumps once in awhile. Living in step with the Spirit who inspired Jeremiah, however, we're also allowed to look through eyes of faith, to see beyond the immediate to what God may have planned. We have permission to trust in God who still wants to "put [his] law in [our] minds and write it on [our] hearts"[1] Along with Jeremiah, we are free to hope in what God can do in the lives of students.

Pastor David Feddes calls it "seeing the unseen." In a devotional on the topic of faith, he writes about faith's power to see beyond the obvious:

> Faith has its own way of seeing. It sees not with the eye but with the heart. Faith sees not just what is happening now but how things will turn out in the end. Faith sees not just people around us but God above us.

1 Jeremiah 31:33

And faith bases its decisions and desires on what it sees.[2]

As I mentioned in the opening chapters, our outlook has an impact on the outlooks of students. Furthermore, because attitudes are partly shaped by what we believe, what we trust in, seeing through the eyes of faith is paramount to heart-centered discipline.

Defying the Law of Nature

Sir Isaac Newton postulated that for every action there is an equal but opposite reaction. Whereas he wasn't talking about people, our sinful human nature seems to operate by this property of Newton's third law of motion. If someone provokes me, my gut reaction is to return the favor. When student mischief seems malicious, that tendency for payback is one of the hardest forces to overcome. In the life and work of Christ, however, we find power to escape this recoil mode; through him we can learn to seek restoration instead of revenge.

If attitudes originate with perceptions, with the way people see, the key to having an impact on a person's attitude is to bump her frame of reference off kilter. Children with negative or malicious attitudes expect others to respond to them with more of the same: spitefulness feeds on spitefulness. When ill will consistently fails to arouse the anticipated re-action, it becomes more difficult to sustain. In his commentary on Jesus' Sermon on the Mount, Dietrich Bonhoeffer advocates for patient endurance over active resistance:

> The only way to overcome evil is to let it run itself to a standstill be-cause it does not find the resistance it is looking for. Resistance merely creates further evil and adds fuel to the flames. But when evil meets no opposition and encounters no obstacle but only patient endurance, its sting is drawn, and at last it meets an opponent which is more than its match....
>
> To leave everything behind at the call of Christ is to be content with him alone, and to follow only him. By his willingly renouncing self-defense, the Christian affirms his absolute adherence to Jesus, and his freedom from the tyranny of his own ego. The exclusiveness of this adherence is the only power which can overcome evil. (p. 141-142)[3]

"Patient endurance" does not imply that teachers allow troublesome students to behave as they choose. Instead, teachers who walk with Christ in the classroom "absorb," as it were, the unkind actions or words of chil-

---

2   Feddes, D. (July-August, 1998). "Seeing the Unseen." *Today: The family altar.*

3   Bonhoffer, D. (1995). *The cost of discipleship.* New York: Touchstone.

dren. In responding they supply not the reaction their students *deserve* but the redirection their students *need*.

The way of mercy is not always an easy road to travel. In today's culture, "an eye for an eye and a tooth for a tooth" still seems an unquestioned precept. Indeed our own egos may condemn us if we don't seek some form of revenge for attack or insult. Teachers of the heart, who choose not to treat discipline as payback, walk this difficult road.

A Space for God

As we near the end of this book, I would like to recall where we began— my first classroom. It looks different now, of course. Not long after I started, that room was combined with the teacher's lounge next door, to house a new central library. Carpenters tore out the thin, makeshift wall which had separated me from the coffee drinkers in the lounge. They also covered up the old brick with drywall and a fresh coat of paint. Yet if I walk into the east section of the library today and look at the small windows, up against the ceiling of the south wall, it doesn't take much to recall what a heat trap that place was in the spring and the fall. I can almost hear the drone of the electric fans as they made war on stickiness and body odor. That old anxiousness comes back, too, as I recall those first students and our frequent struggles with each other for control.

The climate is much better in the space where I currently teach, and not only because of the air conditioning. Yes, I've learned a great deal about heart-centered teaching and correction since moving from that old room. Storms occur less frequently now, and positive attitudes are turning out greater yields. While some classes still bring more instability to the weather than others, those difficult times make the sun even more of a blessing when it reappears.

The gifted custodian who disinfects the desks in my room each week was actually a student in my first class. Though Amy takes her work seriously, she's not beyond sharing an occasional laugh with me about those days of big hair and baggy pants. Confessing how little I knew about teaching back then, I've told her that if I can ever afford it, someday I am going to give our school board a refund on the money they paid me that first year. With my irritability and payback discipline style, the students couldn't have learned anything of significance. Graciously, though, Amy recounts only the kindhearted things she remembers about me as a teacher. Either she is a great liar, or God worked through me despite my failings.

Sometimes our conversations shift to the students of that class—

the places they've moved off to and the vocations they have pursued. Despite their challenges as sixth graders, the majority today are helpful and productive members of their communities. If somehow they could be reassembled in one room, the gathering would include entrepreneurs and managers, medical professionals and counselors, farmers, a cop, an FBI agent, and one janitor—who scares the daylights out of 99.5 percent of all germs known to schoolchildren. More importantly, perhaps, many of these people are committed parents and active members of their churches. Amy's son, by the way, recently occupied one of the desks in my classroom.

In his work on nurturing faith in the Christian school, theology professor Syd Hielema concentrates more on the "believing" aspect of attitudes than on the "seeing-feeling-behaving" angle that I often emphasize. Whereas his rich metaphor of temple building is also different from my climate model, we reach many of the same conclusions. Manipulating morality or emotions, Hielema asserts, doesn't repair the human heart. Only God's Spirit has the power to transform what is broken. And even though our sovereign God can work wherever he wills, hearts are more open to redirection within a community where students feel safe, where questions and ideas are welcome, and where the truth is spoken in love.

One of Hielema's statements on temple construction seems especially fitting here, given the way my first students turned out despite my floundering: "The liberating wonder of temple construction is that it is not our job to change kids' lives. Our job is to build the temple so that children are brought into the presence of God, who will change their lives as he fills the temple." (11)[4] One particular passage from scripture that I have grown to treasure through Hielema's work comes from the book of Ecclesiastes:

> As you do not know the path of the wind, or how the body is formed in the mother's womb, so you cannot understand the work of God, the Maker of all things. Sow your seed in the morning, and at evening let not your hands be idle, for you do not know which will succeed, whether this or that, or whether both will do equally well.[5]

Knowing that God works both through us *and in spite of us* makes it easier to face each new day when negativity and resistance seem beyond our control. Even though the heart remains the center of teaching and

---

4   Hielema, S. (2001, Spring). Making space for God. *Christian School Teacher. 2*, 8-11.

5   Ecclesiastes 11:5-6. In Hielema, S. Ibid.

discipline, we need to trust the Maker of all things to bring about growth and transformation.

Walking with the Master

People who desire to serve more effectively in their calling often search out others who are respected in their field. They highlight sentences in their books or take notes at their seminars. However, if you want to acquire someone's passion, if you really want to see the world through someone's eyes, no form of learning surpasses "face time" with an expert or working at that person's side.

I have acquired the art of storytelling from my parents and other relatives. My pipe-smoking grandfather demonstrated the value in sitting and reflecting. The teachers at Sioux Center Christian School have imparted a passion for excellence in teaching, and they have taught me to see the good in each child. Whereas I continue to learn from people who share their wisdom and time, I most want to pattern my temperament according to the Spirit of Jesus Christ.

While in the process of penning this final chapter, I noticed an unadorned sign in the workshop of the gentleman who repairs our children's musical instruments: "He who sings prays twice."[6] May I share with you the prayer my heart sings as I amble home after long days at school? It is the hymn penned by Washington Gladden:

O Master, let me walk with thee in lowly paths of service free;
tell me thy secret; help me bear the strain of toil, the fret of care.

Help me the slow of heart to move by some clear, winning word of love;
teach me the wayward feet to stay, and guide them in the homeward way.

Teach me thy patience; still with thee in closer, dearer company,
in work that keeps faith sweet and strong, in trust that triumphs over wrong.

In hope that sends a shining ray far down the future's broadening way,
in peace that only thou canst give, with thee O Master, let me live.

---

6 Though I found that Augustine of Hippo is most commonly accredited for this statement, the original source is disputed.

Index

anger 3, 9, 22, 51, 77, 92–93, 95, 97–
    98, 103, 110, 132, 140–41, 147–48
atmosphere 3–4, 7–8, 52, 63–65, 67,
    69–70, 76, 96, 130, 143
  heart-centered 105, 109, 136
attitudes 4–7, 9, 13–14, 17–18, 21–22,
    27, 29–30, 41–42, 46–51, 91–92,
    104–5, 125–26, 139–40, 142–43,
    150
  collective 132, 143
  person's 115, 150
  positive 6, 17, 151
authority 1, 6, 16, 20, 66, 79, 86, 95–
    96, 100–101, 103–5, 136, 138, 141

Baker, K. 25
behavior 5, 15, 20–22, 26–28, 79–80,
    88–89, 91–92, 105, 108–11,
    113–16, 120, 127–30, 132, 138–39,
    147–49
  anti-learning 95
  inconsiderate 119–20
behavior problems 91, 93, 133, 142–43
Belmont, M. 20–21
Bonhoeffer, D. 82, 150
boundaries 17, 28, 92, 96, 107–8, 139
building relationships 34, 40, 44, 117
bullies 46, 99, 107, 128
bullying 79, 119, 123, 125, 128–29

calm 89, 93, 95–96, 100–101, 110, 113,
    126, 133, 138
calmness 29, 97, 99, 101, 103
Christ, followers of 25, 30, 42–43
Christian school 8–9, 152
classroom atmosphere 7–9, 139
  positive 51, 119
classroom climate 4–5, 7, 9, 18, 26, 28,
    30, 38, 46, 116, 119, 125, 136, 141,
    143
classroom community, thriving 49, 57
classroom discipline 105, 117
classroom dynamics, negative 117–18
classroom management 13, 42, 69, 80,
    103, 146
classroom management plans 132
classroom problems 91
classroom rules 40, 70

climate 3–5, 7, 9, 13, 70, 104, 110, 119,
    130, 151
coercion 13, 17, 21, 42, 44, 110
collaboration 55–56, 63–64, 66–67, 124
collaborative atmosphere 63–66, 68–70,
    118, 133, 135, 141, 143
collaborative classroom 63, 69
community 15, 45–54, 57, 91, 119,
    125, 152
complaints 67, 136–37, 143
compliments 16, 43, 50–51
conflict 117–19, 124–27, 129–30, 132,
    138
confrontation 20, 82–83, 93, 102, 109–
    11, 114–15, 117–18, 121, 140
  one-to-one 108, 121, 127
consequences 13, 24, 28–29, 78–81,
    87–88, 92–93, 103, 109–10, 114–
    16, 119–20, 125–26, 128, 135–36,
    140–42, 147–49
  class-wide 141
consistency 2, 15, 21, 70, 104, 109, 116
control 2–4, 9, 11–12, 17–18, 21,
    23–24, 27, 29–30, 66, 82–83, 86,
    95–99, 131–32, 134–35, 151–52
cooperation 13, 28, 47, 53–54, 56–57,
    59, 71, 118
cooperative learning 53–55

defiance 95, 133, 140
detentions 2–3, 13–14, 136
disagreement 57, 125
discipline 26–29, 34, 37, 39, 41–42,
    76–77, 81–83, 90, 92–93, 97–98,
    108–10, 138–39, 141–43, 151, 153
discipline problems 62, 93
discipline situations 4, 80–81, 86
disrupter 98–99
disruption 3, 98–99, 104, 141

emotions 5, 21, 23, 27, 77, 85, 95, 97,
    112, 125–26, 147–48, 152
encouragement 50, 55–56, 92–93, 142,
    147, 149
engagement, high behavioral 21
envy 15, 47–51
evil 29, 150

fairness 49, 80–81, 109, 141
faith 8–9, 36–37, 90, 148–49
  eyes of 37, 149–50
fear 13, 34, 37, 57, 63, 69, 95, 97, 129
Feddes, D. 149
forgiveness 78–80, 126–27

grace 14–16, 18, 38, 52, 78–83, 91,
  104, 115, 128, 148
Graham, D. 82
group, small 49, 130
group work 53
guide 77–78, 148, 153
guilt 78–80, 83, 110, 120

Halbfus, H. 8
harassment 46–47, 117, 125, 129
heart 6–7, 17–18, 20, 25, 30, 36, 44,
  50–51, 77, 94, 109, 113, 124,
  148–49, 151–53
heart-centered classroom 41–42, 47, 52,
  55, 78, 80–81, 93, 104, 110, 118,
  129, 136–37
heart-centered classroom climate 6,
  17–18, 29, 33, 44, 51, 62, 70, 105,
  109–10, 124
heart-centered confrontations 108–11,
  114–16
heart-centered discipline 37, 71, 83, 92,
  109, 112, 119, 128, 134, 147–48,
  150
heart-centered learning 40, 66
heart-centered teachers 21, 29–30, 46,
  48, 81, 83, 89, 92, 94, 109–10,
  113–14, 116, 129, 133–35, 141–42
heart-centered teaching 22, 37, 41, 57,
  63–64, 67, 143, 151
Hielema, S. 152
Hoezee, S. 16
humans 17, 25–26, 30, 42, 63, 70
humor 20, 29, 37, 48, 51, 120, 123,
  134, 137
hurt 25, 43, 92, 114, 117, 119–21, 127,
  129

impatience 89, 91
impatient 89, 91
incentives 4, 13, 15, 17–18, 34
initial patience 89

Jones, F. 95–101, 103–4
justice, restorative 119

kindness 29, 35, 43, 46, 51, 80, 128
kingdom 24–25, 27
Kohn, A. 14, 16

learning community 26, 55, 118
learning experience 62, 65–66
learning goals 14, 54
learning problems 91–93, 114, 133
learning process 62–63, 68, 135
learning tasks 53–54
limit-setting 96–101, 103–5

manipulation 12–18, 104
meeting 82, 116, 125–27, 138–39
mercy 24–25, 147–48, 151
misbehaving students 16, 77, 82, 86,
  96, 100
misbehavior 9, 12, 14, 77–81, 89,
  92–94, 96, 105, 114, 118, 129, 139,
  143
motivation, external 14, 17–18

natural consequences 28, 105, 109–10,
  119, 146
non-patience 89, 91

offenders 103, 119, 128–30
outlook 20, 26, 149–50
outward behavior 5

patience 45, 85–89, 91, 94, 143, 146,
  150
penalty 24, 81, 110, 137, 142, 147
perceptions 5, 21–22, 39, 112, 126–27,
  133, 150
person 2, 23, 26, 37–38, 41, 43–44, 47,
  49, 65, 79, 112, 124, 127
personal confrontations 44, 101, 105,
  116, 121
Piper, J. 43
popularity disorder 34, 36, 38
praise 13–14, 16, 42–43, 50
prejudice 47–49
punishment 4, 14–15, 18, 27, 77, 81,
  87, 93, 96, 104, 118, 147, 149

redirecting teachers 76–77, 115

relationships 23, 27, 34–35, 40, 56, 118, 128, 146, 148
  positive 21, 33–34, 38, 41, 44, 51–52
  teacher-student 34, 44
resistance 20, 25–27, 30, 80, 131, 148, 150, 152
respect 3, 35, 38, 46–49, 52, 57, 65, 69–70, 80, 86, 104, 122, 125, 130, 143
responsibility 17, 53, 56, 79–80, 83, 104, 108, 111, 114, 137
restore 78, 119, 127–28
revenge 24–25, 27, 29, 78, 127, 150–51
rewards 4, 11–15, 18, 27, 50, 83, 96
ringleaders 134–35, 143
rules 46, 59, 67, 69–70, 76, 80–81, 87, 104, 110, 120, 125–26, 132, 136–37, 140, 142

sacrifice 27, 29, 81–83, 93
self-esteem 42–44, 109
shortcomings 38, 40, 80
sin 23, 26–27, 78–79, 93
Skinner, E. 20–21

space 67, 69, 143, 151
stubborn patience 89–91, 94, 97, 116
student classification 36

teachers
  caring 13, 49, 78, 129
  climate-sensitive 4–5
  effective 51, 89, 114–15, 142
teacher tone 64
teaching model for discipline 27–29, 93, 142
troublemakers 117–19
trust 6, 22, 24, 34–36, 39–41, 89–90, 95, 109, 111, 133, 135, 137, 141, 143, 153

Van Dyk, J. 41, 53, 63
victims 119–21, 125, 127–29
Vygotsky, L. 55

Wright, N.T. 25

weeds 45, 47, 145
whole-class setting 108, 121

CPSIA information can be obtained
at www.ICGtesting.com
Printed in the USA
LVHW101436040622
720515LV00004B/53

9 781940 567129